WITNESS TO CHANGE

WITNESS TO CHANGE

FROM JIM CROW TO POLITICAL EMPOWERMENT

Sybil Haydel Morial
Foreword by Ambassador Andrew Young

John F. Blair, Publisher
WINSTON-SALEM, NORTH CAROLINA

JOHN F. BLAIR,
PUBLISHER
1406 Plaza Drive
Winston-Salem, North Carolina 27103
blairpub.com

Library of Congress Cataloging-in-Publication Data

Morial, Sybil Haydel.
   Witness to change : from Jim Crow to political empowerment / by Sybil Haydel Morial ; foreword by Ambassador Andrew Young.
      pages   cm
   Includes index.
   ISBN 978-0-89587-655-3 (alkaline paper) — ISBN 978-0-89587-656-0 (ebook) 1. Morial, Sybil Haydel. 2. Morial, Sybil Haydel—Family. 3. Morial, Ernest N. 4. New Orleans (La.)—Biography 5. African American women political activists—Louisiana—New Orleans—Biography. 6. Politicians' spouses—Louisiana—New Orleans—Biography. 7. African American mayors—Louisiana—New Orleans—Biography. 8. African Americans--Civil rights—Louisiana—New Orleans—History—20th century. 9. Social change—Louisiana—New Orleans—History—20th century. 10. New Orleans (La.)—Race relations--History—20th century. I. Title.
   F379.N553M62 2015
   976.3'35063092—dc23
   [B]
                                2015016054

10 9 8 7 6 5 4 3 2 1

DESIGN BY DEBRA LONG HAMPTON
BACKGROUND DESIGN: ©*Irina_QQQ / Shutterstock*

*Dedicated with love to my children—
Julie, Marc, Jacques, Cheri, and Monique—
who continue to inspire and encourage me
And to my cherished grandchildren, Kemah,
Martine, Mason, Mathieu, Austin, Jaiden, and
Margeaux*

*And, in loving remembrance of my late
husband, Dutch*

Contents

Foreword

Years before the Civil Rights Movement shook the South and our home state of Louisiana, Sybil Morial (then Haydel) and I were just kids growing up in the intimate neighborhoods of old New Orleans.

Ours was a loving childhood. We were surrounded by families and friends who knew we were special blessings from heaven, treated us that way, and demanded that we behave accordingly. It was a blessed life, even in the midst of the bigotry, poverty, and anguish of those years immediately after the Great Depression and the war that followed. Poor people and black people were the victims of an immoral social order that was failing. Yet white people were also caught in the throes of the Depression and the tragedies of a world war.

Looking back, though, living in a struggling society was part of our blessing. We couldn't see our future lives, could not have foreseen how our experiences of sitting on a racial divide would shape where we would go and what we would try to do to change our world.

We were "privileged" but protected. Life was difficult, and we knew it, but we were given the moral, emotional, and intellectual tools to cope with the dangers, difficulties, threats, and challenges. These tools included big families—uncles, aunts, and cousins galore. Our parents entertained each other, cared for each other's children, and created a close-knit community that existed over several generations.

My grandparents knew and respected the Haydels. My father was a dentist. Dr. C. C. Haydel, Sybil's father and our family physician, came to my home to deliver me in 1932, before we had hospitals that we could afford or trust. Our mothers played bridge together in a club called "The Gloom Chasers." In my senior year in high school, I took Sybil as my date to the prom. By then, we had become friends, not knowing our paths would cross again many times in the great movement that was only a shadow yet.

Our fathers had to go north to professional schools. After years at Catholic and Protestant missionary colleges—Xavier University and Straight College, now Dillard University—our mothers became teachers, one occupation open to black women. They couldn't marry young because teachers had to be single.

The disciplined religious values of Roman Catholic nuns and equally dedicated Protestant missionaries from New England formed a challenging and demanding moral contact we dared not question. These were also the years of George Washington Carver, Booker T. Washington, and W. E. B. Du Bois. We were the "talented tenth," who were "blessed" in order to "serve."

These were still hard times, so the dangers of materialism had not yet emerged. We were valued by our "inner worth" and the contribution we made to the community. These principles held amidst poverty, racism, a segregated social order, and a racist legal and political system.

Still, New Orleans was a different South. Centuries of mixed breeding during the French and Spanish occupations had softened the edges of the brutal exploitation of slavery. There was a tolerance, a personal, mutual laissez faire among people, and a constant blending of cultures.

This cultural mix included a strong Jewish community that was just awakening to Hitler's horrors in Europe, a consciousness that created a genuine sensitivity among Jews that opened them to a silent partnership with others who knew oppression.

This cultural gumbo somehow survived in the "sea of poverty" produced by Herbert Hoover's Depression. We became the children of the New Deal of Franklin Roosevelt and the leaders who emerged in the Civil Rights Movement of the sixties. It was not our time yet, but it would not be long.

While intermixing mitigated racism in our New Orleans neighborhoods, we were also repeatedly stunned by stories of the Klan in Mississippi, north Louisiana, and Texas. The first time I saw a Klansman, I was visiting Atlanta for a YMCA conference in the 1940s. Racial violence and furor would make its way to Louisiana in the years to come.

In the crucible of racism and poverty, we either had to lead or drown. Martin Luther King expressed the dilemma in his prophetic claim that "either we will learn to live together as brothers and sisters or we will perish together as fools." By the 1960s, Martin was in the headlines, but Sybil Morial has been on the front lines since her return to New Orleans from Boston University, where she studied with Martin and heard some of his first stirring, visionary sermons.

It is doubtful that New Orleans could have produced two mayors with the dynamic, creative, and visionary leadership of Dutch and Marc Morial without a wife and mother of Sybil's loving strength, intelligence, and moral courage. But the life she lived in the crucible times and her perception of the Civil Rights Movement in New Orleans go far beyond that.

This is her story—a New Orleans story from the inside, and a history of which we can all be proud.

Andrew Young

Acknowledgments

I have many people to thank for helping me bring this book to completion.

First and foremost is my editor, June English, whose professional guidance began with an evening creative-writing course she taught at LSU and, following that, a memoir tutorial. After reading my stack of pages and listening to my stories, she joined me in this endeavor, providing her literary expertise and counsel in giving a voice to my life.

My special thanks go to Carolyn Jackson, who streamlined the narrative and provided historical context for the events of my story. I was touched by her commitment to publishing this memoir. Rosemary James, a journalist I knew from my public and political life, also showed interest in my New Orleans story and introduced me to the literary network of the Faulkner Society and the Words & Music conference. Her introductions included one to Jeff Kleinman, literary agent, who recommended that I send my manuscript to John F. Blair, Publisher, whose excellent staff worked diligently to bring this book to publication. I would also like to thank Donna Brazile, Priscilla Painton, Willeva Lindsay, and a score of other friends who encouraged me to record this story.

A longtime friend, journalist Ponchitta Pierce, edited my initial writings. Her comments were a constant source of encouragement throughout the process.

My continued gratitude goes to Andrew Young, my childhood friend and colleague in the struggle, who generously contributed the foreword to this book.

For technical assistance, I would like to thank our computer/design genius, Jeff Sheldon, along with Kelly Nations, who copyedited the work in progress, and Caleb Nations, who transcribed taped materials.

For research (archival) assistance, I would like to recognize Lee Hampton, Chris Harter, and Andrew Salinas at the Amistad Research Center, as well as Irene Wainright and Gregory Osborn at the New Orleans Public Library, Louisiana Archives Division. They assisted me in gaining access to vital documentation of historical events included in the book. Thanks also to the Xavier University Archives for *A House Divided* and Lindy Boggs photographs. My cousin Curtis Graves provided outstanding photos of the Haydel plantation (Whitney Plantation Museum), as well as a treasure trove of family stories passed down through generations.

My thanks also go to Norman Francis, David Francis, and Don Hubbard, who provided valuable information for parts of this memoir.

And to John and Donna Cummings, who had the vision to create a memorial to those enslaved at Haydel and other plantations.

I am grateful to Dr. Belmont Haydel, my cousin, for researching and recording our paternal Haydel ancestry, and to Dr. Ibrahima Seck, whose scholarly work documented the history of the Haydel plantation, the birthplace of my great-grandfather Victor Haydel, born a slave.

Finally, my thanks to my late husband, Dutch, my partner in the struggle, who was fearless and courageous in pursuing equality and justice for everyone.

White Gloves

It was 1950, and my formal gloves were white. I walked downstairs, through the long hall into the living room, savoring the rustle of my crinoline petticoat and four layers of white tulle. Designed in exquisite detail by a New Orleans debutante *modiste*, the gown was a huge presentation, much larger than myself. I floated out onto our long, tiled porch. Outside, the front garden was awash in bright azaleas, their trumpet blossoms the size of lilies.

A rush of rehearsals, receptions, and parties had preceded this moment. The Sunday before, we had gathered at the ballroom for the first rehearsal. It was the first time we had seen the large room inside the Seafarers Union Hall in the French Quarter. The large lead-paned windows looked out on the bleak docks that lined the Mississippi. On that Sunday, the room seemed enormous, but it was dreary, Spartan, and, most of all, empty. I wondered how we could have a ball in such a place.

The following Tuesday, my mother and I piled my dress and me (in that order) into the car, and my father drove us to the Seafarers Union Hall. The debutantes were called out one by one. On the arm of my escort, a member of the Young Men's Illinois Club whose gloves were as white as my own, I walked as gracefully as I could onto the floor. Once there, I looked up and around—and almost gasped. As in a fairy tale, the gigantic space had been magically transformed. Scrim drapes now defined the abyss, creating a sense of intimacy; massive greenery—trees and flowers—bedecked the hall. Above us hung an orange and blue dawn sky with the remnants of peeking stars.

The queen of the ball made the traditional promenade around the room. The dance, the rituals, seemed dazzling and ridiculous all at the same time. Maybe I knew, maybe we all knew underneath, that the rituals we took part in, a mimicking of a society from which we were excluded, had become hollow. Surely, none of us suspected how the boundaries of that society would soon convulse in this city and throughout the South. Even if we had a suspicion, none of us could have imagined just how deep the wake would cut, though on the surface the first tremors would appear in the simplest of acts:

A little girl would walk through a school door.

A woman would take a seat on a bus.

Students would sit at a lunch counter.

A preacher would have a dream.

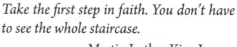

Take the first step in faith. You don't have to see the whole staircase.

Martin Luther King Jr.

CHAPTER 1

My New Orleans

I grew up in New Orleans, on Miro Street, in the Seventh Ward near the London Canal. Ours was a real New Orleans neighborhood with a mixture of rich and poor and everything in between. Two grand houses stood in the block—ours and the one next door, owned by another Negro family. Directly across the street were three single-family homes owned by two white families and another Negro family. A group of shotgun houses, one occupied by whites and two by Negroes, stood down the block. My friend Mona Lisa lived in one of them.

In good weather, we gathered outside. My mother's flower beds graced each side of the large porch and were a riot of colors in all seasons—the bright winter pansies turned over to a rainbow of azaleas and petunias in the spring and orange nasturtiums and red zinnias in the summer. On the porch, baskets of religiously watered, lush ferns sat on tripods among gliders and rocking chairs. People taking an evening walk often stopped to glance admiringly at the greenery and bright flowers as they passed.

My parents bought our house when I was four years old. It was a beautiful wood-frame bungalow, white with French Quarter green (forest-green) trim. Like many homes in New Orleans, ours had an interesting history. It was built in the 1920s by Walter L. Cohen, a freeborn man of color. During Reconstruction, President Warren Harding had appointed Cohen as comptroller of customs for the port of New Orleans. The United States Senate initially opposed the appointment, but Cohen's position was later secured by the efforts of Harding's successor, President Calvin Coolidge. In his time, Cohen was something of a pioneer in race relations. When I was a child, his background was lost on me, but later I came to see its significance as part of my history.

Our driveway led to a huge backyard and an outbuilding that had a garage and a laundry room on the ground level and two rooms and a full bath upstairs, used by the original owner for servants' quarters. The large room served as a playroom for my older sister, Jean, and me. The smaller room held out-of-season furnishings—rugs, draperies, and slipcovers. Light and airy covers and curtains were brought out for the subtropical summers; in the cool, damp winters, we switched to wool rugs and heavier brocade draperies.

There were no playgrounds for Negroes at that time, so my parents turned our backyard into a neighborhood recreation area. It had a paved area and a large grassy place with swings and a sliding board. The girls jumped rope or made necklaces with the four o'clock blossoms that opened—according to their name—at the hour we returned from school. The boys, including my little brother, C. C., played marbles or cops and robbers. A large pomegranate tree in the corner of the yard provided relief from the Louisiana sun. We liked to pick the ripe red pomegranates and crack them open and eat the kernels under the shade. The

Sybil, age one, and Jean, two, in 1933
Author's collection

taste was sweet and sour, and the juice stained our fingers a deep purple.

My mother abided no nonsense in the yard, and we never knew when she might appear in the back door. She would immediately send home anyone who was misbehaving. If her children were causing the trouble, playtime ended abruptly. At the same time, she was pleasant and made it a habit to feed all the neighborhood kids. In summer, on Mondays, traditional washday, she would cook a big pot of red beans and rice. This good-smelling dish, spiced with bits of sausage, pickled pork, and fresh-picked cayenne peppers, would simmer all morning on the stove, filling the air with an enticing aroma. When it was ready, Mother would stand at the back door and call, "Plates!" That was the signal for us to line up, get a dish from the breakfast-room table, and come into the kitchen to get it filled. We all sat on the lawn and ate the noon meal, swatting the greedy Louisiana insects away.

When Jean and I became teenagers, the outbuilding was moved and connected to the main house so that we could have our own suite: a bedroom, a study, and two closets, with a bathroom and recreation room below. My brothers, C. C. and "Cookie" (Glenn), had a bedroom on the first floor next to the breakfast room. Jean and I were just one year apart, and the space suited us perfectly—at least in principle. We were in some ways like twins. In fact, our mother often dressed us in the same clothes, but in different colors. Both of us were readers—Jean read voraciously— and we both loved music. Jean preferred classical, while I loved operettas and lighter music.

My mother, who adored piano music, thought we should learn to play and made us take lessons for years. Once a week without fail, Jean and I would tromp across the London Avenue Canal bridge to Miss Hutton's house. Miss Hutton had earned a master's degree from Oberlin College, a rarity for a Negro student from the South at that time. Her love of music spilled over into her teaching; she offered anecdotes about the composers whose music we learned—Chopin, Mendelssohn, and Strauss. When she admonished us for not practicing (Jean and I often waited until the day before the lesson), she urged us to imagine a picture of what the music conjured up. *Danse Macabre* by Saint-Saens was the regular Halloween piece—creaking doors, rattling bones, scampering mice. When we played *The Skaters' Waltz* by Strauss, we tried to imagine skating on ice, rather a stretch for New Orleans people.

Whatever her method, it worked; her love and celebration of music rubbed off on us. Those years of piano lessons gave me an appreciation and love of music throughout my life, even though, as time would tell, neither Jean nor I had any real talent.

One area in which Jean and I were definitely not twin-like was housekeeping. Like my mother, I was methodical, believing everything had its place—and should be there when I reached for it. Jean, on the other hand, was more of a free spirit and actually quite junky. She resisted making her bed and folding her clothes. Since we shared a room for our entire childhoods, we often fought over the condition of our quarters. At one point, in exasperation, I drew a string across our room to separate us. I can't remember how long that lasted. My mother sometimes intervened in our quarrels and advised us, with an unwavering stare, to "take inventory." By this, she meant that we should examine our own behavior and correct it. And be quiet. Which, facing my mother's grim stare, we usually did.

Jean was five or six inches taller than I, and I looked rather stunted next to her. Oddly, though, she was the one who had problems with walking. Her left leg was deformed from birth. It didn't have the muscle structure of a normal leg, and the foot lacked an arch. So she walked with a slight limp. During her childhood, she had a couple of surgeries—one when she was seven, the other when she was nine. While she was recovering in the hospital, Daddy would always sneak me into her room with paper dolls and crayons so I could play with her. My father, a physician, and mother, a former teacher, were keenly aware of Jean's disability but never treated her differently from the rest of us. She was expected to do chores around our house; things were not made special for her unless it was a necessity. She was never good at sports, but she was a great dancer. The year before my debut, Jean had been chosen queen of the ball. I had watched her practice promenading across the floor, a pretend scepter in her hand.

On Saturdays, Jean and I would get up and dress, then have our usual breakfast of grits, eggs, and smoked bacon. During the morning, we usually worked at our regular chores, cleaning our room and bathroom and ironing our clothes. But on days when our mother had a party, we were assigned special tasks. The duties were specific, depending on whether the event was a formal dinner, a tea, or her bridge-club meeting. If she was planning a reception, for instance, she would call us into the dining room and ask us to set up, pointing out the linens for the table, the serving dishes, and the stemware. We knew what to do; she trained us well.

In the hot afternoons—there was no air conditioning then—we would rest in dark rooms out of the heat, then get up to take a refreshing bath. As the sun diminished, we would emerge, ready to entertain ourselves if we had no more chores.

Because there were few places for Negroes to go out to dinner, my parents often hosted parties at home. Sometimes, my mother ordered flowers or a special dessert, and we would wait for the delivery. The providers of these treats were usually Negro vendors we knew well. The flowers, for instance, came from Haydel's Flower Shoppe, which was owned by my father's cousin. When a centerpiece arrived, we knew exactly where to put the spray on the table.

Like everyone else, our food was rationed during World War II. Still, we paid careful attention to dinners for special guests. Our Sunday family dinners were special also. My mother, like other Negro wives, "made groceries"—as New Orleanians referred to shopping—early mornings on North Claiborne Avenue at the St. Bernard Market. She might prepare a veal roast or a baked chicken with macaroni and cheese, the old-fashioned kind with eggs in the mixture. We always had lots of vegetables—green beans, cabbage, corn, and peas. During the war, some produce—squash, tomatoes, and eggplants—came from my father's victory garden. His handiwork also provided celery, hot peppers, sweet peppers, onions, and herbs—the standard Creole seasonings that flavored everything from gumbo to étouffée.

North Claiborne Avenue was the main street of Negro-owned businesses. A median flanked by huge live-oak trees formed a beautiful canopy. The avenue always teemed with activity. It was home to physicians' and dentists' offices, about five insurance companies, funeral parlors, a busi-

Large oaks provided shade and a promenade area for shoppers along thriving North Claiborne.
NEW ORLEANS PUBLIC LIBRARY

ness school, and a variety of small shops, including retail stores. As a child, I remember being enchanted in one of those shops as I watched a Negro man purchase feathers and beads for his costume. He was one of the famed Mardi Gras Indians. The feathers and beads, along with cords of brilliant colors, would make up the giant headpieces—sometimes extending four or five feet above the head—that the "Indians" wore as they paraded around on Mardi Gras and St. Joseph's Day. Some of the tribes, such as the Wild Tchoupitoulas, were named after real Indian nations. There was sporting competition among the tribes as they paraded. Each tribe had a "Big Chief," who traveled around with a "Scout" and a "Spy Boy"—whose role was to warn the chief of an enemy tribe nearby. These antics came out of traditional stories; many escaped slaves in Louisiana were taken in by nearby Indian tribes.

All along North Claiborne were purveyors of Louisiana specialties. Levada's was the best oyster shop in town. Shoppers could purchase fresh raw oysters or delicious oyster loaves—what we would now call "po-boys"—packed high with rich fried oysters. Mother bought her fresh meat from a Negro butcher in the St. Bernard Market. It was set up much like the market in the French Quarter, its stalls selling meat, fresh vegetables, spices, dry goods, and all sorts of other food items. The market's aroma was an intoxicating melding of Creole and Cajun foods.

Sometimes when my parents were entertaining, we were allowed to go to the movies, escorted by an older relative. Several neighborhood children would join us on the walk to the Circle Theater, which was near-by. Both Negroes and whites could see movies there; we sat upstairs in the balcony, while white people sat downstairs. There was not much traf-fic on the cross streets, but crossing St. Bernard Avenue was a challenge for a parade of children. As we passed the "white entrance," we saw our white neighborhood friends standing in line. We waved shyly to them. We walked around the corner to the "colored entrance" to pay for our tickets. Once, my brother C. C., who was only six at the time, was given the privilege of buying the tickets. He walked up proudly to the window, reached up on his tiptoes to see the cashier, and put the money down, proclaiming loudly, "One aduck and six children!" Jean and I giggled wildly. As we passed through the "colored lobby," each child received a token toy—a Saturday-night treat to encourage attendance. We usually arrived early so we could all sit in one row.

The years before and during World War II were great ones for the movies. All of us kids liked going to "the show." Along with the feature, we saw cartoons and comedies including *Looney Tunes* and *The Three Stooges*. But if the movies featured black actors, it could sometimes be uncomfortable for us. Most of the time, black actors played subservient roles or buffoons—the Uncle Tom scratching his gray head and looking confused, the oversized mammy who chased her foe with a cast-iron fry-ing pan. One black comedian, Lincoln Perry, became a model for later comics including Charlie Chaplin. Even he, though, reinforced the ste-reotype by playing "the laziest man in the world." Such roles were often the only parts offered to Negroes during those times.

Whenever a Negro character was the object of ridicule, the laughter

*My mother, Eudora, with Jean, me,
and my little brother C. C. in 1937*
AUTHOR'S COLLECTION

from the white audience downstairs grew louder. Some Negroes in the
balcony laughed, too, but it always made me tense. I found myself looking down and moving uncomfortably in my seat. Still, the movies were
one social experience that both races shared. The day after the movie, the
neighborhood kids, Negro and white, would get together to talk about
what we had seen.

Members of black society had to make many accommodations.
Since hotels were open only to whites, Negro entertainers and other professional people were housed with New Orleans families who had large
homes with guest rooms, as we did. My father belonged to the National
Medical Association (Negro Physicians), the National Insurance Association, and several service fraternities including the Alpha Phi Alpha
fraternity. My parents, along with other middle-class blacks, out of necessity created our own cocoon of interaction for professional and social

*Standing in our garden in my
Mardi Gras costume in 1939*
AUTHOR'S COLLECTION

activities and at the same time limited the rejection and humiliation we experienced in our Southern cities. These social and professional networks exposed our people to new experiences in accepting venues across the nation and enabled lifelong friendships.

Both my parents also participated in service to the community. Even with my father's demanding medical schedule, he was an active board member of the New Orleans Urban League. He provided gratis medical examinations to all of the Catholic Negro schoolchildren each year, supported black entrepreneurs, and lent financial support to causes he believed in. He was a founding member of the first black savings and loan association, which provided money to Negroes to purchase homes and for business ventures. Such loans were not available from white-owned savings and loans or banks.

My mother, too, was active in our community. She led the Parent-Teacher Organization at our elementary school and took part in auxiliary organizations of the medical association and the Flint Goodridge Hospital for Negroes, the only hospital where Negro physicians could provide care for their patients and perform surgery.

By example, they taught us to respect others and to be of service while we forged our futures in a sometimes hostile world.

We had many visitors to our home, some of them famous. My parents once hosted a dinner for Dr. Charles Drew, the physician who discovered how to separate plasma from whole blood. While whole blood could not be stored for any length of time, plasma could. When World War II began, Drew was put in charge of the United States military's blood supply. However, when orders came down that plasma from Negroes be kept separate from that of whites, Drew was incensed. He insisted there was no scientific basis for such a separation and stepped down from his position.

Just as my parents opened their house to weary travelers, we sometimes stayed with other families. Once, on our way to Chicago, we stopped for the night in Nashville and stayed at the home of a professor at Fisk University, Dr. Horace Mann Bond. His brother Max Bond was a professor at Dillard University and a friend of my father's. We had breakfast with Dr. Bond's family and met a very young—not yet one—Julian Bond. That unassuming toddler became a major figure in the Civil Rights Movement of the 1960s.

Professional groups and fraternities held Negro society together. My father drove all over the country to attend conventions of organizations in which he was a member. Sometimes, my mother traveled with him; occasionally, the whole family went along. Because we could not eat in most restaurants or stay in hotels, my mother would prepare a kind of traveling picnic. We always started out with enough food to last most of the day. If we ran out, we would stop at a grocery store and buy additional fruit, cold cuts, and bread. We'd park off the highway for lunch and give my father a rest from driving. A long trip required more elaborate planning. Where would we be able to buy groceries or stop for the night? Where would we be able to bathe or use the bathroom? This was well before interstate highways, and sometimes the journey took longer than we expected.

It wasn't just the South where black families had difficulty traveling. In 1946, my father went to Detroit for a convention of the National Insurance Association, and he took us with him. My parents, Jean and I, C. C., my cousin Verdun, and A. P. Tureaud Jr. all packed into the Packard. My father had made a reservation to stay at the Book Cadillac Hotel, a nice establishment. We got there a bit late. It was summer and getting dark; we were tired and sweaty from the long trip. I remember all of us sitting in the car while my father walked up the long steps of that grand hotel. Then he came back out. He had a strange look on his face, one I'd never seen before. There was no hint of relief or satisfaction, only sadness.

All I understood then was that I was tired and wanted to go into the nice hotel. But there was no place for us there. My father had been told that the Book Cadillac did not accept Negroes, that it could not honor his reservation. It could not even recommend another place.

Later, I thought that my father must have been upset with himself that he could have been so naïve, that he could have put his family through this humiliation. It was a shock for him. He was aware of discrimination in the North but for some reason had some expectation of civility. Yet even here, we were rejected. I watched him get into the car, determined to find his family someplace to spend the night.

> *Not everything that is faced can be changed; but nothing can be changed until it is faced.*
>
> James Baldwin

CHAPTER 2

Separate, Not Equal

I don't recall when I first heard the term *Jim Crow*. Maybe I grasped its meaning before I knew the term. As I grew up, I came to understand that laws restricting Negroes had existed for a long time. Those laws kept us from going to the nice beaches around Lake Pontchartrain, and to the best parks. They meant we couldn't use most water fountains or sit down for a soda inside a diner in town. They were a given, a part of being a Negro in the South.

Yet people said that the laws were there to make sure Negroes would have equal, though separate, bathrooms, places to play, and ways to travels. In reality, though, Negroes were rarely provided facilities like white people had. The most visible laws required that public schools and public transportation—such as trains and buses—have separate but equal facilities for whites and blacks. This was based on the landmark *Plessy v. Ferguson* case, which originated in Louisiana in 1892. Seeking to test the law against integrated facilities, Homer Plessy bought a first-class ticket on the East Louisiana Railroad and boarded a car for "whites only." The railroad company knew of Plessy's mixed heritage (one drop of Negro

15

blood certified a person's race as black) and was aware that Plessy wanted to challenge the law. He was arrested, and his case made it to the Supreme Court. The court voted seven to one to uphold segregation, mandating the separate-but-equal principle. But the reality was quite different. Negroes continued to ride in the baggage cars of trains and generally in the backs of buses. Segregation continued in the South for many more years until people organized to fight against it.

Growing up, it was a complex task to maintain our dignity within the invisible bars of Jim Crow, but my parents were wise in the ways of the world. They set an example in the conduct of their own lives for what they wanted us to learn. Still, I was a teenager before I really understood—in an emotional way—what being a Negro meant, even in a mixed city such as New Orleans. My parents told us that things would get better. They said this every time we had to drive past a nice beach or a restaurant and not stop. They tried to reassure us, but it was hard to continue believing.

All the schools I attended in New Orleans in the 1940s were for Negroes. This separation was true for public, parochial, and private schools. It was the law of the South.

There were no eighth grades in the schools then, so I and several other students applied for and passed a test to determine whether or not we were capable of high-school work. Those who passed went straight to Xavier Preparatory High School at the age of eleven.

Besides being young, I was small (my mother said "petite"). Jean, the tall one, had a Buster Brown haircut, which I greatly envied. Because I was much shorter and covered with Shirley Temple curls, people thought Jean was much older than me.

At Xavier, as was true of all the Catholic schools I attended, I was taught by Blessed Sacrament nuns, all of whom were white, and by lay teachers, who were both white and Negro. The Blessed Sacrament order of nuns had been founded by Philadelphia heiress Katharine Drexel, who dedicated her life and fortune to establishing a religious order for

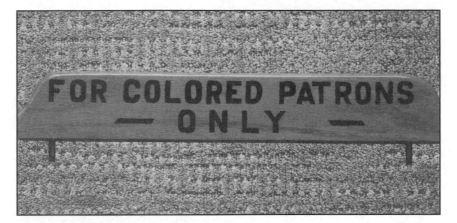

Segregation sign used on buses and streetcars
COURTESY OF DON HUBBARD

the special mission of educating American Indians and Negroes. Just as my parents had high expectations of me and assured me that I was as good as anyone else, the nuns and lay teachers at my schools reinforced those same values. This attitude countered the scorn and diminishment we received on the street.

Until we began Xavier Prep, Jean and I never had to ride public transportation; our parents had a car. Now, the ride to school—two buses and a streetcar—took us close to an hour. With this transition to high school, friendships between whites and Negroes all but disappeared. All of us rode the buses and streetcars to our schools, but we were separated. We Negroes sat in the back of the bus behind the "For Colored Patrons Only" moveable screen, while whites sat in front of the sign. If our white neighborhood friends were on the same bus going to a white school, we didn't speak or even acknowledge each other.

It would be another decade before Rosa Parks took a "white seat" on a Montgomery, Alabama, bus because her "feet were tired." That action rocked the South's order of precedence—on the bus and in every other public place. I would not attend school with white students until I went north to college in Boston. In the meantime, we were Negroes, and no matter how we dressed, talked, or thought, few whites saw us as more than "colored."

As children, we wore school uniforms obtained from local sources; buying our other clothing in downtown department stores presented challenges. Sometimes, salespeople ignored us and served several white people before turning their attention to us. On one occasion, my mother took me shopping in one of the downtown department stores. We selected several dresses and asked where the fitting rooms were. The saleswoman said, "You can't try on the clothes, but you can buy them and bring them back if they don't fit."

I suppose she thought this was a courteous compromise.

There were no Negro store managers, cashiers, or even salespeople. Negroes were always relegated to menial jobs, such as janitors or short-order cooks at downtown lunch counters. There were few, if any, public restrooms for us. Very rarely, we would find a restroom labeled "Colored"—and even then, there was no gender differentiation. Because of this barrier, we had to prepare ourselves before leaving home. As we dashed through the door, my mother would call out, "Go to the bathroom, please."

Seating was an issue nearly everywhere we went. My mother loved the opera; performances were held at the New Orleans Municipal Auditorium. Jean and I accompanied her to several operas—*Carmen* stands out—although we were required to sit in the "colored section" way up in the crow's-nest, from which the characters on the stage appeared miniscule. What I remember most about those outings is not the beautiful music and costumes but the many steps—103—we had to climb to the colored section; Jean and I counted them every time. When we reached the top, we bent over in exhaustion. Mother paused at every landing, and when she reached the top, she, too, was crippled from exhaustion—and anger, which faded only when the opera began.

New Orleans offered not just art in performance but also fine arts and architecture. From much of this, we Negroes were also excluded. City Park, built in the mid-nineteenth century, was one of the largest municipal parks in the nation. It was not far from where we lived, and we often walked or rode our bikes nearby, but not in it. One hot, humid summer day in 1947, Jean and I and future Atlanta mayor Andrew Young were riding our bikes along Esplanade Avenue with some other teenagers from the neighborhood. There were maybe a half-dozen of us. As we reached the end of the avenue, we were facing City Park. A canopy of giant magnolia trees a block long led up to the impressive Delgado Museum of Art. Broad steps and lovely columns stood at the entrance of the building. Just to the right of the drive was a cooling lagoon under oak trees. We were hot, and the shade of the drive was enticing. We also wondered what was behind the museum, so we ventured in, relaxing out of the sun among the lush green trees and lawns.

We barely had a chance to stop before a policeman in uniform appeared seemingly out of thin air. He was alone and had a billy club in his hand. We had been joking and chatting as we pedaled along, but we quickly quieted. He looked menacing, and his voice was rough. He shook his stick at us.

"You little niggers get out of here. You know you have no right to be here. Get out, now!"

We turned our bikes around as fast as we could. When we got a safe distance out of the park, we stopped to catch our breath.

Andrew looked worried. "Our parents will be upset if we tell them what happened. We know we're not allowed in the park."

"Well, I'm mum," Jean said.

"Me, too," I said.

The others repeated the promise.

We didn't say a word about the incident to our parents until years later. By that time, the morality of the rules, and of breaking them, had a whole new meaning. Jim Crow was on the run.

Wealth or privilege did not spare you from the indignities and . . . [humiliation] of southern laws and practices. You were reminded every day as you went about your ordinary routines that you were less than second class.

John Hope Franklin

CHAPTER 3

Riding with Jim Crow

When we were young girls, my cousin Adoria and I used to dream about taking the train all by ourselves to visit her grandparents in Franklin. Louisiana had a much more complex system of rail stations at that time, and Franklin was located three hours away from New Orleans, just above Bayou Teche. We would talk with serious anticipation about this trip with our uncle Morris, who told us that a large mechanical crane carried the train across the Mississippi. Adoria and I were so engaged with this idea that by the time I was an adult, I had converted it into an actual memory. Our parents, though, would never have consented to let us travel alone.

I was a teenager on the verge of starting college in Boston before I took a train trip by myself, all the way from New Orleans to Boston.

The night before, my mother reminded me, "Take a lunch to eat at your seat on the train."

My father lifted his head from behind his newspaper. "You can have your dinner later in the dining car. The laws have changed, and you can eat at a table. The conductor will come through the cars to announce

The Southern Railway terminal in New Orleans, circa 1950
ALEXANDER ALLISON COLLECTION, NEW ORLEANS PUBLIC LIBRARY

dinnertime. The dining car may be several cars toward the back. You will have to walk through."

Unlike the dreamt trip to Franklin, this journey would be a long one, about twenty-five hours. I awoke at six in the morning to a mild gray day and dressed for the trip in a navy-blue suit. I brought my hat and white gloves downstairs—de rigueur attire for female travelers in the 1950s. My luggage was already at the door, ready to be put in the car. Once it was stowed, our whole family piled in; Mother, Daddy, Jean, C. C., and Cookie would all accompany me to the train station for the eight o'clock departure. I was exhilarated to be traveling all by myself on the train.

The Southern Railway station was a grand building on Canal Street, the main downtown shopping street. The street was lined with upscale shops and variety stores including Woolworth's. In the 1950s, Negroes were permitted to shop in the stores but not to sit at the counter to eat.

Jean, C. C., my mother, Glenn, and I pose as we wait to leave for the train station for my first trip alone, 1950.
AUTHOR'S COLLECTION

My father parked the car. He and C. C. carried my luggage to the colored waiting room to check it. We had to enter the station through a door around the corner on the side street. The arched doorway that led to the main waiting room was for whites only.

The Negro porter greeted us warmly and called my father "Dr. Haydel." Daddy doffed his hat and said, "It's nice to see you this morning."

The white waiting room was visible from the colored waiting room; the clerk behind the counter served both white and colored customers. The white waiting room was larger and brighter and had new-looking benches; the benches in the colored waiting room were dull, worn, and scarred.

We walked out on the platform, and there was the *Southerner*, the sleek steam train that traveled the route from New Orleans to New York.

It was nearing eight, and another porter on the platform was encouraging people to continue walking along the track to cars farther down. When he saw us, though, he held his hand to the first car behind the engine, indicating where I should get on. "Step up and board the train. It will be leaving shortly."

I hugged my family and kissed them goodbye.

As I boarded, the porter directed me to turn right at the top of the steps. There, I found I was in the back half of the baggage car. When I turned to look for a seat, I realized they were filling up quickly with what appeared to be only colored people. I sat in a seat next to the window. Soon, I heard the porter shout, "All aboard!" and the train began moving slowly out of the station. It was exciting to be moving on the train. I looked around and smiled at the people, who smiled back at me. I moved my light baggage and settled in for the long ride to New York.

Soon, a white conductor came through the car to collect our tickets. The rhythm of the train on the tracks was soothing as I looked out the window at the changing countryside from Louisiana into Mississippi. The train went by small towns with one-room stations and farms where I spotted fieldworkers tending to the crops. They all seemed to be Negroes. The conductor stuck his head into our car and called out the station stops in Mississippi: *Laurel, Hattiesburg, Meridian.* Around noon, I ate some of my lunch. Everyone else in the colored car seemed to have brought lunch as well. The aroma of fried chicken made my bland ham and cheese sandwich seem boring.

Hours passed as we made stops in Alabama and Georgia. At about five-thirty, I wanted to go to dinner, but there had been no announcement about the time. I stepped into the next car, looking for the conductor, who had not visited our car since collecting our tickets. He came rushing from the car ahead, blocking my way.

Before he said anything to me, I asked, "What time is dinner being served?"

He coughed slightly and said, "Now."

"How far back is the dining car?"

He sputtered something I couldn't understand and then said, "About four or five cars back."

I slipped past him and crossed through the doors between cars. Reeling through car after car, I finally came to the dining area. The diners were separated in a most unusual way. Negroes wishing to dine on the train were assigned to one table at the end of the dining car, next to the kitchen. A curtain was drawn around the table after we were seated so the white people didn't have to look at us. We ordered from the same menu and were served by the same waiters; they were all Negroes, as were the chef and other kitchen personnel. The waiter who served me was attentive, deferential. Something in his face, though, seemed to express regret in having to serve me behind a curtain.

We spent the night sleeping upright in our seats. I woke to see the sunrise peeking through tall buildings as the train passed through the cities of Philadelphia, Trenton, and Newark. The *Southerner* arrived in New York at Penn Station at about eight-thirty in the morning. I was not sure where I would board the train for the rest of my trip. I went to the information desk and learned I would have to go to Grand Central Station to board the New York–New Haven–Hartford Railway train to Boston. I retrieved my luggage—there was no porter in sight—and took a taxi to Grand Central. I picked up a snack and went through the bustling waiting room to the correct platform. As I boarded the train, I was surprised to see that I could sit in any car that had a vacant seat.

My return trip from Boston to New Orleans provided another strange ordeal. At Penn Station, I boarded the *Southerner* for New Orleans. I sat in a car for both white and colored people. But as soon as the train crossed the Mason-Dixon line—in Maryland, the border state into the South—we colored people were moved. Again, we occupied the baggage car, where a wall separated our seats from the half of the car reserved for baggage. I was back on the train with Jim Crow. I settled down in my seat and thought, *I dressed up in my hat and gloves to sit in the baggage car.*

Soon, air travel would become a common means of transportation. Inside airports and on airplanes, there was never discrimination or segregation. The sky was unlimited.

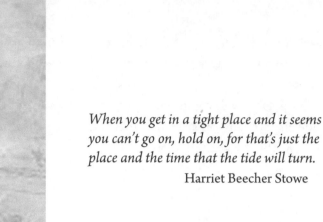

*When you get in a tight place and it seems
you can't go on, hold on, for that's just the
place and the time that the tide will turn.*

Harriet Beecher Stowe

CHAPTER 4

Storm

Six months after my debut in New Orleans, I was standing with Jean on the deck of the SS *Roma*. It was an exceptionally dark night. The sky was black. There was no sign of anything except our ocean liner in the middle of the inky Atlantic. The passengers didn't know it, and maybe the crew didn't either, but we were sitting on the edge of a hurricane.

That year, 1950, was a heavy one for tropical storms. The United States Weather Bureau recorded thirteen of them in the Atlantic. Though spawned in the warm seas, only four made landfall on the Gulf Coast or in the Caribbean. The rest made their way—a few all the way from the African coast—across the Atlantic and then northward, spinning their violence out in colder seas. Though the New England fishing season was severely impacted, land dwellers took little notice. Ships at sea, however, were troubled by the storms, especially in August and September, when one after another thrashed the shipping lanes between Europe and North America.

Troubled is a kind word for it. I know this because Jean and I were on one of those ships, crossing from Cherbourg, France, to New York City.

The jet age had just begun. Sea travel, while longer, was more luxurious and comfortable, though maybe less adventurous. Or so we believed.

Jean and I were packed in with 848 other Catholic college students returning from a tour of Europe. The trip was a gift from my parents—a remarkable gift, really, since the two of them had never traveled abroad. For me, it was something of a celebration; I was getting ready to embark on one of the big adventures of my life, moving north to finish my undergraduate education at Boston University.

I had completed my first two years at Xavier University in New Orleans, still under the care of the sisters of the Blessed Sacrament. Xavier was a great place to be during those years—so small that I knew most of the student body, and yet a college with a great social life. We all participated in festivities surrounding football, basketball, and track. After the games, there were hops. We jitterbugged to rhythm-and-blues in our bobby socks and loafers.

Xavier was an intimate place, yet the teachers addressed all students as "Miss" or "Mister" (I was "Miss Haydel"), giving us a dignity and sense of propriety we didn't have on New Orleans buses and streets. The intimacy was nurturing and reassuring, but I longed to be somewhere different. While New Orleans is—and was—one of the quintessential "different" cities of the world, it was my home. I loved it, but I knew it. And I wanted to know somewhere else, to know myself in another place. The trip to Europe was a first immersion in the outside world.

Six Negroes were on the tour—Nora Pierce, Rosemarie Christophe, Jean, and I from Xavier; our cousin Belmont Haydel from Loyola in Chicago; and Mary Hines from Boston. We were a curiosity among Catholic students from the Northeast, the Midwest, and Canada, who had not encountered Negroes at school or in their neighborhoods or social circles. Jean and I, who were light brown, were asked if we were Spanish. My first response was to laugh, but I stifled it.

Still, I was stunned by the directness and curiosity of a fair-skinned red-haired student named Alex from Upstate New York, who asked, "Do you tan?"

"Yes," I told him. "I get darker brown in the sun."

I tried to be polite, but my friend Nora was vastly more assertive. She was dark-brown skinned and twice our age. She was the center of attention in one of the common rooms our first day on the Atlantic.

"And just what island are you from?" I heard one student ask her.

Nora raised her almond eyes, and I could see mischief in them. "Island? I'm not from any island."

"Not from an island?"

"No, I am from New Orleans. New Orleans, Louisiana."

The student backed up and was silent, but Nora persisted.

"Why would you assume I was from an island?"

An uncomfortable silence followed.

The curiosity was not limited to Americans. When we were in Rome touring the Vatican museums, I was walking with Nora and some other students when a group of German tourists approached Nora and touched her hair as if she were a doll.

In heavily accented English, one asked, "Where are you from?"

The group's guide and interpreter clarified the question.

Nora's eyes sparked. "I am a Negro from the United States."

The interpreter translated again: "Did you pay for your own trip?"

"Of course I did," she said sharply.

"Where do you live?"

"I live in a large house in New Orleans, Louisiana."

Incredibly, another question was asked and translated: Did she own it?

"You bet!" she said. It was a phrase that was unlikely to be translated, but the tone was perfectly clear.

Still the questioning continued. Did many Negroes own their own homes?

"Yes, many Negroes own their homes and live quite well."

Five years after World War II, consciousness of the diversity of Negro life in America was nearly nonexistent.

Racial discomfort aside, the voyage to Europe—with stops in Paris, Rome, Venice, Florence, and London, as well as excursions to the healing springs of Lourdes, France, and St. Francis's home in Assisi, Italy—had been pleasant and without incident, and the return trip promised to be much the same. The weather was balmy for the first days of the crossing. About midway across the Atlantic, however, the afternoon seas roughened and the skies turned from pale blue to slate gray. The next morning, even before we ate breakfast, the bell signaled an emergency drill. The eerily loud sound was accompanied by an announcement that all passengers, without exception, needed to come on deck. We had experienced a couple of other drills since leaving France, but this one seemed oddly urgent.

Jean and I lined up along with the rest of the passengers to receive our life jackets. We put them on and went toward our assigned area on deck. By now, the rocking of the deck made it difficult to get anywhere. As the ship tossed and turned, we held as tightly as we could to a railing. If we couldn't reach a railing, we held on to someone who had hold of one. After the drill, we returned to "normal," going back to our cabins. But then the ship began to rock even more violently. The PA barked an order not to go on deck. Jean and I didn't say anything, but I could see fear on her face, and I felt my own tighten. We tried to go back to our diversions. Shuffleboard and Ping-Pong were off limits because we couldn't go on deck, so we settled for table games such as cards, checkers, and backgammon. Even they proved a little tricky because the ship kept shifting.

The next morning, Jean and I were hungry. We made our way through the tilting halls to the dining room. Though the seas had done no damage to our appetites, most of the rest of the passengers were less stalwart; the majority were nursing seasick stomachs in their cabins. The dining room was filled with empty chairs, so Jean and I had plenty to eat—breads and pastries, cheeses, fruits, and some kind of cereal, maybe polenta. It wasn't my favorite. I spooned my portion onto Jean's plate. We had been told to drink lots of fluids on the trip, so we downed multiple glasses of apple and orange juice.

That night, once again, the dining room was all but empty. However, our appetite for Italian food remained undiminished. Jean and I forked bowlfuls of pasta and sauce into our mouths and continued to dessert. If we were going to die, we would at least die satiated. Soon, we heard an announcement on the PA for all passengers to report to the common rooms. It sounded ominous. Nuns and priests served as chaperones throughout the trip. At the end of the meal, one elderly priest began to pray out loud. In a solemn tone, he recited a prayer of absolution, a ritual of forgiveness reserved for near-death circumstances. Jean and I stared at each other; maybe the chaperons didn't think we were going to make it. Shortly afterward, the ship's engines cut off. We were still tossing in the waves but going nowhere. Later, in many of the common rooms, nuns and priests prayed with each other or with students.

Nora had not felt well enough to come to the dining room, but she said she thought she could abide some bread and water. After dinner, I clutched my way along the wall to Nora's room, bread and water in hand. She opened the door for me, and I saw the tumult inside. Everything had fallen or slid onto the floor. I smiled at Nora, who didn't look quite well but was putting up a brave front. I was about to say something when I heard small squeaks emanating from the side of her bed. I bent over and saw two Pekingese puppies sitting in a newspaper-lined box. I remembered her whispering to me as she was coming aboard that she had the puppies. I knew she had spent considerable time admiring the toy-breed dogs in Paris. They weren't popular in the United States yet. I couldn't believe she had actually smuggled two live dogs onto the ship.

"How did you get them in here?" I asked. I reached into the box and lifted one out. They were so soft and adorable.

"It was easy. I just carried them in a basket, smiling. No one told us what we couldn't bring on the ship."

Nora was nearly always perky, but the waves had taken their toll on her. She barely managed to choke down the crusts of bread I had brought her from dinner. However, after downing a bit of water, she reached for one of her bags and brought out a bottle of French wine—more contraband she had gotten aboard.

As I was eyeing her bounty, the ship swayed, and I slipped off the chair to the floor. Nora reached down and helped me up with one hand, the wine bottle clutched in the other.

"I bought this wine for a later celebration, but this may be our last." Her face was strangely serious, and I suddenly had a chill. "This will help us sleep," she said, opening the bottle.

But sleep was way down the road. For the next two hours, Nora enthralled me with what are known in New Orleans as "graveyard stories"—stories of dark romance and intrigue. My Catholic conscience told me to plug my ears and run, but Nora was a great storyteller, and she talked without intermission. At one point, as the ship mercilessly swayed, she took out a lovely rosary she had bought in Rome and gave me one she had bought for her daughter Ponchitta. "We must pray," she said.

And so we prayed, but afterward the risqué stories continued, interspersed with advice about men—about whom she had pointed opinions. For her era, she was a liberated woman, but she was practical in her marriage counsel.

"Sybil," she warned me, "don't fall in love with the first handsome man that comes along. Those handsome men will bring you grief. Some men will marry you because they think you are rich. Look out for those gold diggers. You find someone who may become richer than you, and always keep your secret stash of cash."

Her spiraling tales then went down another dark lane of memory, keeping our minds off our impending doom. I came out of her room red faced but enthralled. Would a priest's absolution cover this?

I stumbled back to the quarters I shared with Jean and tried to sleep as the ship continued to toss. When we awoke, though, the vessel was still. We dressed and went into the dining room; the seas were calm. We heard the engines of the ship restart.

Miraculously, we were going home. We were also going to get a shower. Through the whole hurricane ordeal, water had been rationed. We had to line up for showers, and if we weren't close enough to the front of the line, we had to wait another day. Jean and I finally got a brief shower two days before we landed. After drying off, I struggled to get into a now very tight dress.

Upon reading the weather reports, I realized that we had eaten our way through not a single hurricane, but two. It was my first experience of the power of natural violence—but not my last.

As the seas settled, so did our nerves. Our lives were spared; now what? I began to think about Boston again. I spent my last night on the now-quiet seas tossing and turning and agonizing about being late for my first semester at Boston University.

At a breakfast of eggs, cheese, bread, and juice the next morning, I leaned across to Jean: "I wonder if BU will even let me register. Classes will already be started. I will have missed an entire week of school."

"You worry too much. They'll understand that it wasn't your fault. Really, Sybil, you don't have any control over a hurricane. When they hear your story, they'll feel sorry for you. They'll want to know what happened."

I sipped my orange juice. It tasted sour. "Does this stuff taste bad to you?"

"No. It tastes like orange juice."

"I don't know one person at BU."

"You'll be fine. You always are. You just need to get there and figure things out."

A few hours later, we received a wire from our parents, who had come to New York to meet us:

WILL MEET YOU WHEN YOU DOCK IN NEW YORK.
WILL BE HAPPY TO SEE YOU.
MOTHER AND DADDY

Getting the message relieved me. I knew that once I saw them, I would be okay.

Jean and I didn't actually spot them until we disembarked. They were standing behind two other couples. We ran to hug them. As I embraced them, I felt my worries ease.

Our mother took one look at our full cheeks and our skirts straining at the seams. "You both acquainted yourselves with Italian cuisine, I see."

Jean and I blushed, guiltily remembering the bowls of spaghetti we had shoveled into ourselves.

But I had other things on my mind. All at once, I blurted out, "What if I can't register now? I'm late for school. I'm late for everything. What will I do?"

My father wrapped his arms around me. "Don't worry about this, Sybil. I went to Boston and registered for you. It's all taken care of."

I raised my eyebrows; my mouth hung ajar. I stared at him in disbelief. Registering at Xavier had been fairly easy, but BU was a huge university. I couldn't believe he had accomplished it.

He saw my skepticism. "Yes, Sybil. Everything is taken care of. All of your courses and your housing are in place. You'll have to catch up on your classwork, of course. Your father can't do everything for you."

I laughed. I would make it through the academic hurricane, too, it seemed.

Jean and I spent the next hours luxuriating in baths, scrubbing the SS *Roma*'s dirt off of us. The best thing about being ashore, aside from seeing our parents, was being able to run a full bath and acquaint ourselves with a fresh bar of soap.

*Now is the accepted time, not tomorrow,
not some more convenient season. It is
today that our best work can be done and
not some future day or future year.*

W. E. B. Du Bois

CHAPTER 5

North

The day after I stepped off the SS *Roma*, I was on the train to Boston. My mind passed from one frantic thought to another, but eventually I settled into the rhythm of the rails, remembering some of the travels I'd taken with my parents as a child.

My parents tried without exception to be civil with people and to avoid confrontation. They had to be polite for our sake, for our safety. But I think they must have been angry sometimes. I think that most people who are discriminated against hate it, hate the exception, hate the scorn, the feeling of inferiority. Growing up in the Jim Crow South, subjected to its segregation and subjugation, I knew such practices were unfair, but I had to keep quiet, too.

No matter how I looked at it, I was a Southern girl. I had spent almost my entire seventeen years in New Orleans. And while New Orleans wasn't a typical Southern city, much of what was customary and reliably Southern existed there, and I among it.

I had some fairly specific expectations of what my future might hold.

I wanted a husband and children, a family like the one I'd grown up in. I also wanted a career, at least at the start. Given that I was a Negro, I knew—and had accepted—that I would have limited choices, even with an excellent education. Of these, teaching seemed my best option. A lot of women who were teachers managed to raise families and continue to work. Teaching would put me in an environment that offered flexibility. During my years at Xavier, I had developed close ties with the nuns and lay teachers who instructed me. These honorable people had given me a sense of possibility, and now I wanted to express that in the world. There was honor in teaching.

I had been just fifteen when I began my senior year in high school, and I wanted to attend college somewhere other than New Orleans, maybe even outside Louisiana. But my parents counseled me to wait a couple of years, so I enrolled at Xavier. Early in my sophomore year, I wrote to several colleges in the Boston area. I had read a lot about the city; its historical and academic richness fascinated me. By the time I brought it up with my parents, I had decided on Boston University, which had a strong teacher education program. My mother urged me to consider Wellesley College, but I politely rejected the suggestion. Wellesley had no teacher education program at the time, and I wanted to begin working as a teacher immediately after graduation.

I applied to Boston University and was accepted as a transfer student. Xavier was strong in the liberal arts, and I had accumulated more than enough credits to merit junior status. I would graduate with my class. When I boarded the train at New York's Grand Central Station, I was told to get off at the Back Bay Station in Boston, which was close to my dormitory. I gave the address to the cab driver: 4 Charlesgate East.

When I stepped out of the taxi, Charlesgate Hall loomed over me, covering an entire short block. Its limestone structure with turrets and bay windows conjured up memories of European castles I had just seen. The foyer and the first-floor parlors and offices all had high ceilings and

Charlesgate Hall in the snow, above the Charles River.

Greek columns; the building's one elevator brought it into the twentieth century. Charlesgate Hall was a bit forbidding, but I knew I would get used to it. After all, this would be my home away from home. I would grow here, and I could sense that. The little pink-frocked girl who played jacks with her neighborhood friends on the veranda would soon be replaced by a young woman, one with new expectations, connections, and ideas that could never have been forged in the South.

All along as I grew up, a subtle resentment had been brewing in my head, although at first I barely recognized it. My family, especially my parents, tried to reassure me about my separation from the white world and thereby, to a degree, stalled my bitterness. "One day, things will be different," they would say. "Our day will come."

But while life races by briskly when you are an adult, a child's days stretch out endlessly. While in unspoken and spoken ways my parents conveyed a sense of hope for a more humane society, I grew impatient.

Why, I wondered, *should my color separate me from the things I want to see and do? Why can't I get a drink of water at the fountain? Why can't I use the public restroom when I need to? Why can't I ride the Ferris wheel in the park? Why can't I go to the nice beach? Why can't I go to school with my white friends? Why do we have to sit apart at the movies?*

In Boston, I discovered for myself a whole new world where everything public was available to everyone. This new world provided fodder for my imaginings. My Southern guidebook on "What a Negro Woman Can Do" began a process of revision. *I can go to that restaurant and order my lunch. I can try on that dress at Bonwit Teller. I can sit wherever I want on the bus. I can go to the museum. I can get good seats at the opera. I can. I can.*

I had an urgency to see everything—right now. Even though I had fleeting spells of homesickness—gumbo was an unknown commodity above the Mason-Dixon line—I relished my new life in Boston. I would always have an abiding love of Louisiana, but in leaving it, I had found that my roots could grow both deeper and wider. In 1950, I was alive in a whole new way. I could meet new people—people from different ethnicities and religions, people from different parts of the country and the world.

Indeed, the roommate assigned to me was Izetta Roberts. What a thrill to find out that Izetta was from Liberia in West Africa! Right away, I was intrigued by her lilting accent. I did not know much about Liberia or Liberians, but I was fond of Izetta from the start. She had traveled from the same continent from which my ancestors had come. Yet she had grown up with a kind of freedom I had been denied in the United States.

We had long conversations not only about Liberia but also about other African nations, some of which had recently gained independence from colonialism. In her country, President William Tubman had just been inaugurated for a fourth term amid much pomp and circumstance. Izetta's father had served in the Liberian Senate. I was intrigued by her descriptions of the inaugural events, but it would be many years before I

Izetta and I lounging in our dorm room, 1951. She introduced me to African cultures, and we became friends for life.
AUTHOR'S COLLECTION

began to understand the complex nature of Liberian politics.

Our suite mate at "the Castle," as our dorm was called, was Eunice. A graduate student from Puerto Rico, she told us much about her island's beauty and culture. In Spanish tradition, she carried both parents' surnames; she was Eunice Alvarez de Choudens, the latter being her mother's surname. This cultural point raised another subtle awareness in me of the acknowledgment of women as equals.

Izetta was quite sociable. She became my gateway to meeting students from all over the world. She belonged to the International Students Club in Boston, whose members included students from Nigeria, Ghana, Ethiopia, Lebanon, France, and other countries. She invited me to the club's social activities. I was excited to meet students from such diverse backgrounds. Ketema hailed from Ethiopia, Fawzi from Lebanon, and Pierre from France; all of them brought unique cultural and political sensibilities to our serious discussions. They also enlivened our entertainment with ethnic dancing, food, and art.

I was expanding my relationships, going beyond an environment comprised of people just like me. Although New Orleans was diverse, most of my friends had been Southern, Negro, and mainly, but not exclusively, Catholic. In Boston, there were Negro students from Atlanta, Jacksonville, Birmingham, Memphis, and Richmond, as well as New Orleans. They attended not only BU but also Harvard, MIT, and Boston College, and we socialized through national fraternities and sororities. (I had been initiated into Alpha Kappa Alpha at Xavier and continued in that sorority at BU.)

⚜

Among the other new experiences for us students from the South was cold weather. When the first snowfall came, Izetta and I went across the street from the dorm to the Fenway and frolicked in the snow like children. The strange, almost eerie quiet muffled the sound of nearly everything but the car tires on the streets. On the rare occasions when it snowed in Louisiana, children and even adults would come out and frolic. Here, though, few people were out—just those going quickly to their destinations. For Bostonians, snow was no novelty and required sensible preparation. Harvey, a friend on his way to his dormitory, stopped to tease us and tell us that the snow was wet and we needed hats. We hadn't thought about the snow as frozen rain, which would melt shortly and drench us.

There were other revelations about clothing and weather. When a relative in Puerto Rico learned that our suite mate Eunice was coming to

Boston to study, she loaned her a fur coat to counter the brutal climate. The coat was skunk fur and was rather pretty to look at, but when it got wet, it stank to high heaven. On freezing cold and wet days, Eunice continued to wear the coat. Knowing we were in store for the skunk odor until the coat dried, Izetta and I dreaded Eunice's return to our suite.

For us Southerners, though, there were other, more significant lessons to learn. The experience of freedom crystallized into a sense of what was possible for the South, for what it could become. We dreamily talked about change—and for the first time, the talk carried the savor of genuine hope. We were aware of court challenges to the laws of the South. Through Negro newspapers such as the *Pittsburgh Courier* and the *Afro-American*, we kept up with the progress of the challenges to segregated schools, even though we had to travel to Roxbury, a community where many Negroes lived and had small businesses, to buy those papers. With great interest, we watched for news of a major court decision.

At the end of my junior year (my first at BU), the dean of women called me into her office and told me that she and the administration wanted to show support for racial mixing in the dormitory and set an example for students to follow. In 1951, "diversity" was not generally a goal or even discussed. The dean asked if I would serve as a counselor and room with a white student on one of the freshman floors. Izetta and I had become dear friends and had planned to room together again, but reluctantly I agreed to the dean's request.

That summer, I returned to New Orleans. It was fun being back with my family. As a treat, my father planned to take Jean and me out on his boat. A couple of times a month, he would launch at the fishing areas on the New Orleans lakes or on the bayous and marshes in the Mississippi Delta. He now had an attachment on his car to connect the boat and trailer and had come up with the idea that Jean and I could water-ski. Getting out of the summer heat and on the water was an enticing idea. Jean and I were fairly jumping with excitement as Daddy hitched the boat to the car. In a few minutes, we pulled out and were on our way to Lake Pontchartrain.

We stopped at Seabrook, the only area on the lake where Negroes were allowed to swim and boat. He backed up to an area where he could let down the boat into the water.

Neither of us had taken lessons in water-skiing. This was still the early 1950s, and the era of beach and bikini films was a decade away. But we were game. First, we had to figure out how to get up on the skis. Learning how to stand up while the boat was moving proved a challenge. The next step was to position yourself with the skis pointing upright. Then, as the boat gained speed, you pulled yourself up. All of this required some serious leg strength.

Jean went first but fell immediately into the water. She tried again, but still no luck. I watched as she toppled again and again. As hard as she tried, she just could not get into a standing position. Her one leg, malformed from birth, was too weak. Looking sodden, she finally got out of the water. "Your turn, Sybil."

I had learned a few things watching her, but on my first and second tries, I, too, flopped in the water. On the third try, though, after wavering slightly, I started sailing. Lake Pontchartrain is huge, and Daddy took me on a long ride. It was a great feeling of exhilaration—moving fast with the wind and spray in my face.

Eventually, we stopped, and I came back to the shore and toweled myself dry.

"That looked like fun," Jean said, then turned away.

⚜

In the fall, Jean and I went to Boston. She would enroll at Simmons College to pursue graduate work in library science. It was a great choice for someone who loved books as much as she did.

When I returned to "the Castle," I met my new roommate, Janet Blasnack. She was a senior like me and had impressive credentials; she was both a Phi Beta Kappa and a fraternity queen. This was my first opportunity to be close to a white person from the North—Norwood, Massachusetts. Janet was as curious about my life as I was about hers. We got along well. Although we carried out our responsibilities as freshman counselors, we were not happy about the noise and the constantly ringing telephone outside our room. This was before dorm-room telephones and long before cell phones.

Janet invited me to spend a weekend at her home, and I accepted and met her parents. When she married, she asked me to be a bridesmaid, but I had committed to being a bridesmaid in another wedding on the same day. It seemed as if everyone was getting married at that point. Sometimes, I wondered when that would be my destiny, but I was in no particular hurry.

During my senior year, I made friends with Jeanne Martin, a graduate student in music education from Camden, South Carolina. Several of us from Charlesgate Hall went on an outing at a roller-skating rink. Back home, there were no rinks for Negroes; we skated on the public sidewalks. Having been deprived of this activity in the South, Jeanne and I took wild advantage, flying around on a flat surface until we were near exhaustion. We finally collapsed on a bench.

What began as a breathless skating outing turned into an intense conversation and the beginning of a lifelong friendship. Here we were, two girls from the Deep South in one of the premier cities for the arts. The Boston Symphony Orchestra, the Boston Pops, and the Boston Opera Company were all there for the taking. Museums and live musicals and dramas abounded, and we didn't have to climb a hundred steps to see them. Thrilled to enjoy what had been denied us in our Southern settings, we attended as many concerts as we could afford. Because Jeanne was a student of music, she shared her knowledge of the composers and their works. I even began to enjoy Wagner, and German composers in general.

Together, we expanded each other's social lives. While still an undergraduate, I attended a party at the Negro Business and Professional Men's Club Hall, a venue where Negro students and young people gathered for sorority and fraternity socials. There, I met Martin Luther King Jr., from Atlanta. Martin was a serious graduate student intent on completing his doctorate. He had a charming personality and—most importantly—a car, a rarity in the 1950s. Martin dated Jeanne for a short while and hosted a going-away party for her when she completed her graduate courses in January. I think Martin was seriously interested in Jeanne for a time, but she had other ideas.

When Martin came to study for his Ph.D., he was already an ordained minister; he often served as guest preacher in Boston-area churches when the presiding minister was out of town. Martin was no more than twenty-three years old then, but we in Charlesgate had heard that he was an extraordinary preacher. When the buzz in the dorm was that Martin was going to preach at Columbus Avenue Methodist Church or Ebenezer Baptist Church, we all rushed to the service. Even at his young age, he was a gifted speaker, and his messages were soul stirring.

One Sunday, I went to early Mass so I could join my friends and hear Martin's sermon. It was worth the effort of getting out of bed, for he preached a memorable text that morning. This was long before the women's movement, but he extolled the great contributions women had made to society. I remember clearly his deep voice intoning, "Woman is a gre-e-a-a-t institution!" He infused this pronouncement with so much emotion it seemed to shake the church benches. He talked about our resourcefulness, our compassion and loyalty, our strength, and our courage. It was something I had not heard before, and it made a strong impact on me. I had never really felt limited because I was a woman, but Martin's sermon stirred a pride in me—a pride in my gender and a resolve to set

A master's graduation party in Boston in 1953 for my friend Jeanne Martin, hosted by Martin Luther King Jr. and his roommate, Philip Lenud (both seated). Clockwise from Martin are Eloise Jones, Ida Wood, Jeanne Martin, Ken Simmons, and Mable Carter. Sybil stands in the middle.
AUTHOR'S COLLECTION

my goals higher. I began thinking of the constraints placed on women because of tradition.

While a doctoral student, Martin began dating Coretta Scott, a graduate student at the Boston Conservatory of Music. She was a warm person, pretty and utterly dignified. He fell hopelessly in love with her, and after that we hardly saw him. Coretta complemented and balanced Martin's captivating personality. He had found the woman he was looking for, the woman he needed for his life. Coretta and Martin married in 1953.

Martin, of course, was Baptist. My education in other Christian denominations was to be expanded by my dorm mate and friend Harriet Jones, whose father was a bishop in the Pentecostal Church. Harriet and I had extended conversations about our respective churches. She eventually invited me to spend the Thanksgiving holiday with her family in Philadelphia. Her father was hosting a regional conference at that time. Since I had never attended that type of church, I was curious. I agreed to accompany her to one of the special services there.

As it began, Harriett leaned over to me and whispered, "I forgot to tell you that our services are very spirited."

It was a good thing she alerted me, so I wasn't entirely surprised when people began to shout and dance and speak in tongues. I sat frozen, trying to grasp what I was witnessing. The service, needless to say, was in vibrant contrast to the reserved rituals of Catholicism.

In the early spring of my senior year, my academic advisor, Dr. Helen Murphy, offered me an assistantship—if I began graduate studies in the fall semester. I was torn because I was anxious to get a job and become independent, but I accepted. About that time, the placement office in the School of Education announced that teams from a number of school districts would come to prospect for new teachers. Since I would be going to graduate school, I was not job hunting. Still, I decided that I would interview, if only for the experience. Since it was just practice, I thought, *Why not interview with the best?* So I signed up with representatives of two of the most prestigious public school districts, in nearby Newton, Massachusetts, and Scarsdale, New York.

The next day, I got a message that the placement officer wanted to see me.

"You need to know," he said, "that these school districts will probably not consider hiring a Negro, and I don't want you to be disappointed or embarrassed."

Having grown up in the Deep South, I was not intimidated by the possibility of rejection. I had lived with it all my life. So I was relaxed during the interviews, knowing it was not do-or-die.

The next week, I was invited for a second, group interview before the top administrators of the Newton Public School District. We had started as seventy-five candidates; now, there were just seventeen of us. The administrators went around the room and asked each of us why we should be hired. I was comfortable with the questions and gave details of my travels within the United States and in Europe.

A week later, I was offered a position teaching first-graders. I said I needed a few days to think about it.

When I spoke to Dr. Murphy about it, she said, "Sybil, any teacher would give her eyeteeth to teach in the Newton Public Schools. It's one of the best districts in the nation. How can you pass up that opportunity? Don't turn it down until you have given it a lot of thought." She added, "I doubt if there are any Negro teachers in the entire school district. I will gladly release you from your commitment to serve as my assistant."

I was grateful for her understanding and encouragement. It was an incredible opportunity; now, I could accept without regret.

As to the placement officer who had cautioned me about the possibility of rejection, when I informed him about my offer, he apologized for his comments and wished me well.

So I became a first-grade teacher by day and a candidate for my master's degree by night.

While I was a senior at BU, Jean was studying library science at Simmons. In 1953, a university physician took an interest in her problem leg. He said he had discussed it with a colleague who was on the cutting edge of reconstructive surgery (a term not then in general use). Jean agreed to see him. After his examination, he said he believed surgery could improve the function and appearance of her leg. He consulted with my father by telephone, and they agreed to meet when Daddy came to Boston for my graduation. My father, the surgeon, and Jean agreed to do the operation right away, while the family was in Boston.

The surgery went well. After three days, the family returned to New Orleans. Jean's recovery, though, would last at least a month, so I stayed with her during those weeks. She read all day except when we—she on crutches—went to Boston Common. It was close to our rented rooms and also near the doctor's office. We would sit on a bench in the June sun and then take an early dinner at a nearby restaurant. I kept in touch with our parents, reporting on Jean's recovery.

We were all hopeful that the surgery would improve her condition, but in the end there was little change. She was quiet on the train ride home to New Orleans, reading, as she often did, most of the way.

The lawyers argued [in Brown v. Board of Education] that the history of segregation laws reveals that their main purpose was to organize the community upon the basis of a superior white and inferior Negro caste.

John Hope Franklin

CHAPTER 6

Meeting of Minds

On May 17, 1954, I came home from my teaching job in Newton to an apartment I shared with Doris Sewell and Barbara Roundtree. Neither of them was home, so I turned on the radio to listen to some music. What I heard was something else, some astonishing news: the United States Supreme Court had ruled unanimously in the case of *Brown v. Board of Education of Topeka* that racial segregation in the public schools was now illegal!

A burst of hope overwhelmed me as I thought about that victory. Victory had eluded us so often. I was on an emotional high and could not think of what to do with myself until my roommates came home. I called my parents and Jean to share our joy. For days, we talked about it endlessly with each other and with every Negro friend.

What would this really mean? Would all the schools in New Orleans be open to all children? Would the decision by the highest court in the land make it happen? After the ruling, we Negro students from the South—Atlanta, New Orleans, Birmingham, Jacksonville, Memphis, and other cities—had conversations about the emerging New South. We talked about leaving the freedom of the North to return home and become involved in the changes. I don't think any of us knew exactly what that would entail, but we were determined. A large wall that had surrounded us all of our lives now had a good-sized chink in it, and we could envision it, like the walls of Jericho, tumbling down. Our strategy had not yet developed, but we experienced genuine excitement and a real feeling of hope.

⚜

The following summer, I met Ernest Nathan "Dutch" Morial. I use the word *met* because until then we knew each other only in passing. Years later, we would discuss how we remained on each other's periphery for so long. I had been a student at Xavier for two years at the same time Dutch was; he was a year ahead of me.

I had just returned to New Orleans from Boston for summer vacation. All my New Orleans teacher friends had started vacation a month earlier, but I had taken a two-week accelerated graduate course as part of my master's degree in education at Boston University. As soon as I got settled, I called my friend Lydia Sindos and asked what was on the social agenda.

"We're having a Great Books social," she said. "It's at my house tonight. Come on over."

I was delighted by the invitation. Two summers earlier, a few friends and I had tried to join the Great Books Club at the New Orleans Public Library and were rejected. Apparently, we didn't have appropriate pigmentation to read great books. So we had organized our own Great Books Club. Those evenings were fun, in addition to being intellectually stimulating, and we got to choose our own great books. The volume on the agenda that night was W. E. B. Du Bois's *Souls of Black Folk*. Du Bois, like a few powerful black rhetoricians who would follow him, had a sense for the peculiar experience—and power—of black women. "But what of black women?" he wrote. "I most sincerely doubt if any other race of women could have brought its fineness up through so devilish a fire."

We finished our book discussion and continued our social time until about ten o'clock. At that point, almost everyone had left except Dutch Morial and another young man. I hadn't really noticed Dutch during the evening. However, as we slowly made our way out, the three of us began an intense conversation about *Brown v. Board of Education*. I was struck by Dutch's verve and sassiness. He wasn't like the other men I knew, black or white. We went on talking for a while and then decided that, even though it was late, our discussion needed to continue. There weren't many choices for Negroes at that time, so we went to a black nightclub. It was an unappealing place, really. I couldn't believe I was there, that he had taken me. But he was intent on the discussion, and we talked until very late.

At midnight, Dutch said, "This discussion is not over. To be continued tomorrow."

I was intrigued. I wanted to know this man. His every word seemed to testify that he knew who he was and where he was going. By all accounts, he was direct and ambitious. The previous February, he had completed requirements for his law degree a semester early, making him the first Negro to graduate from the Louisiana State University Law School. His entrée into the dorms three years earlier along with another black law student had been greeted with shouts of, "Niggers in the dorm!" Yet he had survived and was eventually befriended by several of the other law students.

Dutch had just begun practicing law in the office of A. P. Tureaud Sr., the revered dean of Negro attorneys in Louisiana. Dutch didn't mention any political aspirations; in those days, Negroes were not expected to have any. It was still difficult—in some places impossible—to register to vote in the South, much less run for office. Something in him, however, seemed undaunted by all of this. Maybe he sensed that times were indeed changing, or maybe he was just braver than the rest of us.

Years later, I would hear a story about Dutch as a young man, long before the Civil Rights Movement began. In those days in New Orleans, the screens on buses proclaiming "For Colored Patrons Only" were placed in holes on the backs of seats and could be moved forward and back. Negroes had to sit behind the screens. On occasion, just for devilment, a Negro student would sit in front of the screen. Almost immediately, the driver would stop the bus, walk up to the student, snatch the screen, and demand that he or she move to the back of the bus. On more than one occasion, a Negro student picked up the sign and flung it out the window. Inevitably, he was put off the bus.

I was told this story by two friends who witnessed it. One day, Dutch was riding the bus home from high school. He was sitting alone, in a seat directly behind the screen. He was light skinned for a Negro, and a white passenger, thinking Dutch was also white, picked up the "For Colored Patrons Only" screen and moved it behind him so that he was in the white section. Saying nothing, Dutch moved the screen back in front of himself. The passenger stood once more—this time in an agitated state—and moved the screen behind Dutch again.

"You belong in front of the screen," the white passenger insisted.

Dutch grabbed the sign and again placed it in front of himself. "I know where I belong," he said.

The day after our Great Books meeting, Dutch called and asked if he could come over so we could continue our discussion about the significance of the *Brown* decision. I said yes.

A few hours later, he was in our living room.

"Do you know how far reaching this can be?"

I looked at his intense face and felt his sense of determination.

"It may go far beyond the schools," he said. "The process may be slow, but change has begun."

We were both full of hope. This was the most significant event for our people in our lifetime.

Later that evening, Dutch said, "I heard that the hundred-member Tulane faculty overwhelmingly adopted a resolution recommending admission without regard to race. There's an editorial in the campus newspaper in agreement."

That got me to thinking. I knew that Boston University would accept six credit hours toward my master's requirements from another accredited university. Even then, the Tulane student body was quite cosmopolitan, with many students from other parts of the country and from Central and South America. I could enter as a Negro student and test the waters.

"Do you know when the summer session starts at Tulane?"

"Monday, I think," Dutch said.

"How about my trying to register for two courses at Tulane? All they can do is tell me Negroes aren't allowed. What do you think?"

He nearly leapt off the chair. "Do it," he said.

There was a hitch in my plan to go to Tulane. First of all, I had not applied or registered, much less been accepted, at what was a competitive institution. That by itself could give the school reason to turn me down. Still, I decided to give it a try.

Bright and early on Monday morning, Dutch called to wish me luck as I headed for Tulane. I met with the dean of the graduate school; I explained that I had just arrived in New Orleans and wanted to enroll in two courses at Tulane. Without hesitation, he advised me to have Boston University wire my transcript. I could attend the classes of my choice and formally register when my transcript arrived. He suggested that I check with his office each day.

This is too easy, I thought. Still, while I was pretty sure it wouldn't last, I dove in. Each course met every day, and I actively participated in the class discussions and became friendly with a few students. One professor was curious about my origins and asked a few probing questions: "Where are you from originally? Where did you get your college degree?" One by one, I deflected them.

Each day, I went in to see if my transcript had arrived. Upon learning of my situation, one student offered me the use of his library card. I had been in classes for three days. On Wednesday after class, several students invited me to join them in the cafeteria for lunch, but I declined, thinking that my presence could cause trouble. Eating with Negroes was still taboo in the South. The students insisted, however, so I agreed. My presence elicited a few stares but nothing else.

After lunch, I went to the dean's office. My transcript still hadn't arrived.

At the end of each day at Tulane, I shared the events with Dutch. He reassured me that every hour and every day I remained meant progress: "Your presence exposes them to a peer who is a Negro, and many of them never knew or have even thought about Negroes as equals."

On Thursday after class, I went to the dean's office, and he asked me to come in and take a seat. I thought, *This is the end of the line for me.*

"Your transcript has arrived, Miss Haydel. Please complete this registration form."

I looked down at the paper. One of the items to be filled in was race. As I wrote "Negro" in the blank, I wondered why he hadn't asked me to fill in the registration form the first day. I returned the form.

As he perused it, the dean began a monologue: "Miss Haydel, your academic record is impressive, and you are the caliber of student Tulane is interested in. Unfortunately, we cannot accept you because Tulane does not admit Negroes."

He went on, "Paul Tulane, the founder of the university, specified in his will that the university was established to educate white males. White females attend the sister college for women, Newcomb. They can attend graduate courses at Tulane."

He discussed no options for Negroes. I did not interrupt him as he plodded on. He did seem uncomfortable justifying the situation.

I went immediately to the public telephone and called Dutch. "It's over," I said. "I was asked to leave."

"We knew the end would come. You have some spunk. I admire that. Why don't you go over to Loyola University and try to register there?"

I took a walk over to Loyola, just a short distance away. I was a Catholic, but the process of rejection went even more quickly than at Tulane. I was told immediately that "according to state law, Negroes cannot attend the same schools as whites."

"What about the recent Supreme Court ruling outlawing segregated schools? That is the law of the land," I said quietly.

The dean insisted that the state law was still in effect and had to be adhered to. He dismissed me by saying, "I hope the laws will have changed by the time you are ready to pursue your doctorate."

As I walked out of his office, I wondered if he actually meant what he said. But it was perhaps naïve to think that a century's worth of Jim Crow laws, not to mention centuries of slavery, could be overturned in a moment, or a year. We would need patience—as well as other skills—for this fight. The barricade that kept us out of schools, jobs, restaurants, hotels, and even restrooms would have to be dismantled brick by brick, law by law. I had no idea how bloody our fingers—and other parts—would get in the process. It would be nine years before Negroes were admitted to a Tulane graduate program, as a result of a lawsuit filed by Negro students Barbara Guillory and Pearlie Elloie. It was argued by a white supporter of civil rights, attorney Jack Nelson, and underwritten by another Caucasian champion of equality, Rosa Keller.

Dutch and I continued to see each other. He would come over to my house; he seemed to enjoy being there, especially with my mother.

Well into July—after we had been seeing each other practically every evening for six weeks—Dutch turned to me. "What would you say if I asked you to marry me?"

I was taken aback by his politic *if*. I paused for a bit.

"You can't have a trial run," I said. "I'll answer you when you ask me."

Sing a song full of the faith that the dark past
    has taught us,
Sing a song full of the hope that the present
    has brought us.

James Weldon Johnson

CHAPTER 7

Love and War

It was late August 1954. On the weekend before I returned to Massachusetts to finish my master's degree, Dutch gave me his fraternity pin. It wasn't exactly a romantic moment, but he did actually attach the pin to my blouse without stabbing me. For the times, being "pinned" was something like the engagement before the engagement. I could see that he was working himself up to the actual event.

After I returned to Boston, he wrote his first letter to me: "Sybil, although I did not give you my frat pin in a romantic manner, I am asking you to consider it as our engagement symbol until I can do better."

I hesitated to write him back, but not because I wasn't interested, as I most definitely was. I just couldn't manage to tell him that, in less than twenty-four hours, I had already lost his pin. I had worn it on my jacket as I traveled to Boston. When I got to my room, I looked for the gold, Greek-lettered bar. It was no longer on my jacket. I looked in my bags, up my sleeves, in my pockets, anywhere it could have fallen, but to no avail. I was beside myself with angst. He was a proud member of the Alpha Phi

Alpha fraternity. His membership, and the pin he had given me, meant a lot to him. I sank into grief and resolved, at least for the time being, not to tell him. After two days, I finally confessed on the phone. He didn't say a word. And no wonder. Dutch was already worried that I would find Harvard men to date while he was miles away; the nearly immediate loss of the pin just proved that I wasn't serious about the relationship. He most definitely was.

We also had other obstacles to cross. The Korean conflict had not yet come to a close, and young men Dutch's age were still being drafted. It was a hard time for him. He did not want his career detoured, and he wanted to be close to me. In his letters, he discussed alternatives that would shorten his service time and possibly offer a better experience. Given his legal background, he wrote to the air force and the navy about a commission in the judge advocate general's (JAG) section. He even sought support from his congressman, F. Edward Hebert. Before any of them replied, though, he was drafted into the United States Army and ordered to report for duty the day after Thanksgiving.

I had been back in Boston only a short while. Now that Dutch's whole life was being turned upside down, though, I had no choice but to go home for Thanksgiving.

The first thing on his agenda was, in the old-fashioned way, to ask my parents for my hand in marriage. He was a bit nervous, even though he had spent considerable time courting my mother at home in New Orleans while I was in Boston. He continually hung around our house, trying to get information on other bachelors I might be dating, worrying about "those Harvard boys," and trying to get a chance to talk to me on the telephone when I called home. My mother was genuinely fond of him, but Dutch was apprehensive about the confrontation with my father.

In the end, all went well. When Dutch asked for my parents' blessing, he received it. My father saw Dutch as an up-and-coming profes-

My engagement photo, taken with Dutch in 1954
NOLAN MARSHALL, PHOTOGRAPHER

sional. He thought, prophetically, that Dutch had a bright future.

Our spirits fell on the day after Thanksgiving when it was time for Dutch to leave. It was cold and gray in New Orleans as we made our way to Municipal Auditorium for Dutch's induction. He had no idea where he was being sent or what he would be assigned to do. Afterward, his mother accompanied us to the train, so there was no opportunity for an intimate goodbye.

Dutch's six weeks of basic training—from November to January—would be conducted at Fort Gordon in Augusta, Georgia. He wasn't looking forward to it. We began exchanging letters immediately, but his were sad. In one letter, though, his spirits lifted. An agent from the Counter

Intelligence Corps (CIC) had interviewed him. If he were accepted, he would be assigned to school in Baltimore, Maryland, for several weeks. After that, he would have several choices of assignments, either foreign or domestic. He wrote of other advantages to the position, the most important being the possibility that we could be together after CIC training.

At Christmas, Dutch got a leave and came to New Orleans. There, he presented me with a beautiful diamond ring, and we became formally engaged. I managed to keep tight hold of this pledge.

In January, after waiting some weeks, Dutch was accepted into the CIC program. He would begin his schooling in March 1955. He heard through the grapevine that previous classes of CIC graduates had been sent by President Eisenhower to Vietnam. The United States was not yet engaged in the civil war there, but it seemed that "intelligence" was under way, and advisors, including CIC staff, were serving in the country. When Dutch first heard about this prospect, he had me bring out a map so he could see where Vietnam was. Like most Americans, we didn't know. Our country was just concluding its involvement in Korea. We were worried that he would go to Vietnam for a year-and-a-half tour, instead of to Korea. Whatever happened, chances were he would be sent overseas for an extended period of time. We decided to get married right away.

In February 1955, I was still teaching in Newton, so we had a small wedding in Boston's Back Bay at St. Cecilia's Church. I wore a white ballerina-length gown and carried a bouquet of stephanotis. My parents, Jean, and Cookie came up from New Orleans. Several childhood friends (including Sylvia Tureaud, as well as Valda and Preston Jenkins, who served as matron of honor and best man) joined my Boston colleagues (including the superintendent of the Newton Public Schools) for the ceremony.

Miraculously, Dutch and I were able to add a short honeymoon in Washington, D.C. It was an exciting time for us to be in our nation's capital. It's hard to believe now, but it had been a segregated town until 1954.

Now, its doors were suddenly open. We visited the Capitol, the House and Senate chambers. From the balcony of the Senate, we watched Lyndon Johnson in action on the floor. At that point, he was the Democratic majority leader, and it was clear he was destined to acquire even more power. He was such an operator! We watched him intently as he convinced his colleagues to vote for a piece of legislation he was promoting. He moved steadily, going from one colleague's desk to another, leaning in, whispering some important detail. Then he moved up to the podium, found some notes, and went back for another round. It was fascinating to see. We also spied Margaret Chase Smith, who was the only woman in the Senate at that time. A Republican, she was one of the few who had spoken out for the right of free speech during the McCarthy hearings just a few years earlier: "American people are sick and tired of being afraid to speak their minds lest they be politically smeared as 'communists.' . . . Freedom of speech is not what it used to be in America."

At night, we feasted on lobster at Harvey's Restaurant, went to plays at the National Theatre, and danced at the Casino Royale.

When Dutch completed intelligence training, we were relieved to hear that he would be assigned to Fort Holabird in Maryland for the rest of his military tour. After gaining tenure, I resigned from my teaching position in Newton. When school closed in June, I moved to Baltimore to be with Dutch. I had a husband now and a new life. I was offered a teaching position in the Baltimore Public Schools and was assigned to School Number 94. (I could never understand why public schools were given such cold and impersonal numbers, instead of the names of historic or prominent local people.)

Maryland was in legal terms a Southern state. Its schools had been desegregated for students the previous fall after the historic Supreme Court decision. In 1955, I was assigned to one of the schools selected for faculty integration. Five Negro teachers joined a faculty of twenty-six whites. The student body was about 70 percent Negro. The name of the white principal, Elizabeth Storm, did not exactly represent her style. She was a tall, gray-haired, and attractive woman with a strong voice, and I found her to be a no-nonsense administrator who was fair, patient, and compassionate.

One of the white first-grade teachers, Johanna, was from Mississippi. She was in Baltimore because her husband was stationed in the service nearby. She was friendly to me and to an Asian teacher, Gertrude Natori, from Hawaii, whose husband was a medical resident at Johns Hopkins University Medical Center. Johanna had written and illustrated a booklet especially for her class that she thought would thrill the Negro students. It was about a little Negro boy named Jigaboo, whose mother said to him every night, "Jigaboo, Jigaboo, Jigaboo Jam. You is my sweet li'l black honey lamb."

I was taken aback. I asked why she chose the name Jigaboo, and she said, "I think it is a cute name for a little black boy." (*Black* was not yet an acceptable term for identifying our race.)

I realized that her choice of that name was a result of her upbringing in a segregated environment in which Negroes were sometimes caricatured. I told her that *jigaboo* was a derogatory term in the Negro community. She said she didn't know that, and I could see that she was embarrassed and would think twice before showing the book again.

A white third-grade teacher referred to me as a "Negress" and to a Jewish teacher as a "Jewess." I gently told her that those terms were not acceptable and suggested that she use *Negro* and *Jew*. She told me that she had never in her life worked with, or really known, a Negro or a Jew and didn't know any better.

Phyllis Mirkin, the Jewish teacher, and I became lasting friends. Long after we left Baltimore, I learned from Phyllis that one of the other teachers had said in the faculty room that she was going to be nice to the Negro teachers, but she would *never* eat with them.

Dutch came to meet me after school one day, and Doddril, one of my white students, asked me if Dutch was colored. After I said he was, Doddril asked, "Then how come he gots the same color skin as me, and I am white?" I told Doddril that Negro people came in many shades. Dutch didn't like being taken for white. He was proud of his black roots.

These incidents demonstrated to me that the separation of the races in the South fostered stereotypes of Negroes and prevented both whites and Negroes from learning about each other. This was probably the first time that the white Southern teachers had interacted daily with Negroes who were their peers, and conversely it was my first adult day-to-day interaction with white Southerners.

Baltimore was still a segregated Southern city. Its public facilities were not open to Negroes, but only forty miles away, Washington's had now been desegregated. Dutch and I drove there as often as we could. We went to watch Congress, to the theater, to restaurants, to sidewalk cafés, and to our favorite nightclub, the Casino Royale. When the cherry blossoms were in bloom, we went to the Tidal Basin and to the national monuments. Together, we enjoyed the new freedom and openness in our nation's capital. And we enjoyed each other.

In Baltimore, we lived in a cottage on the property of Dr. Joseph and Flavia Thomas, whom we met through my New Orleans friend Sylvia Tureaud. It was only eight minutes from Fort Holabird. The Thomases' home had once been a whites-only country club. The beautiful white clapboard house was surrounded by shade trees, flower gardens, and a fishpond situated on Bullneck Creek, which led into Chesapeake Bay. Our little cottage, adorned with red tulips in the spring, was a virtual fairytale setting.

I liked the tulips but wanted some perennial flowers to last through the season. I gathered up some replacement plants and one day began pulling the tulips. Mrs. Thomas saw what I was doing and began to cry, "Oh, Sybil, Dr. Thomas loves his tulips!" I thought I was in real trouble, but he never said a word about the tulips.

Truly, Joseph and Flavia were surrogate parents. Joseph was full of humor and common sense. Once when I had referred to my father as "Daddy" in front of Dutch for the umpteenth time, Joseph cajoled me, "Sybil, you are a married woman. You have a new Daddy now." Flavia was warm and wise and had a keen mind and a generous spirit. She was from Houma, Louisiana, a small but colorful town just north of the Gulf of Mexico. She told wonderful, earthy stories about her home there. Joseph's lucrative medical practice was in Dundalk, the Baltimore suburb where his home was located. Atypical for the South, he had both white and Negro patients. He often noted, "There is no difference in my black or white patients. They are all red inside."

Few Negroes owned a yacht in the 1950s. But Joseph had an eighty-four-foot boat named *FlaJoe* (a shortened version of their combined names). This lovely extravagance was docked just behind their house. It slept ten and had a working galley. Both Joseph and his wife could navigate the yacht. During spring and summer, they took it out for two- or three-hour spins into Chesapeake Bay, inviting friends—including Dutch and me—and extended family to join them.

On one special outing, the plan was to rendezvous with two other boats of friends at a designated spot in the Chesapeake near Fort McHenry. The fort was a great historic monument where the Star-Spangled Banner flew during the War of 1812, which inspired Francis Scott Key's anthem. The three boats idled near each other, close enough so we could talk from deck to deck. After a short time, we started back home. The other boats had sailed out of sight when the *FlaJoe* started its engine. The motor caught, then sputtered out. Soon afterward, we tried to use the ship-to-shore radio to report our distress. It malfunctioned. We were stranded on the Chesapeake. Our hope was that a passing ship would recognize our plight and send for help, but we were too far from other craft to be seen. The atmosphere on the *FlaJoe* was now tense; Flavia and others were praying. One of the guests, Mrs. Patterson, saw

Flavia quietly reciting the rosary and said to her, "Pray another one and another one, Flavia!" Finally, just before dark, the Coast Guard got word and came to rescue us. We were taken to Annapolis, the nearest port, and eventually got back to Dundalk by bus. We later learned that another vessel had spotted our darkened boat in the dusk and alerted the Coast Guard.

I still savor the memories of our time with the Thomases. It was like a year-long honeymoon for us, but it came to an end when Dutch's stint in the army was up. He was eager to return to practicing law and to what he thought was his destiny. I resigned from the Baltimore Public Schools, and we traveled back to New Orleans in September 1956.

We didn't realize it then, but it was not the city, or the South, we had left behind.

Storm clouds are gathering
The wind is gonna blow . . .

Maya Angelou

CHAPTER 8

The South Quakes

When Dutch and I returned to New Orleans in September 1956, we had high hopes. The Montgomery Bus Boycott had begun the previous December and was still under way. Rosa Parks had boldly taken a seat in the front of a city bus and catalyzed the movement. The boycott was sponsored by the mildly named Montgomery Improvement Association. But it was not mild. As the boycott began, Martin Luther King was elected its head and mobilized it. He was barely known in the South then, but his great rhetoric took hold: "I want it to be known that we [will] . . . gain justice on the buses in this city. And we are not wrong. . . . If we are wrong, the Supreme Court of this nation is wrong. If we are wrong, the Constitution of the United States is wrong."

Dutch was eager to resume his civil rights work and to build his practice alongside A. P. Tureaud, whom he deeply admired. Tureaud had been challenging separation laws since the 1940s. His first significant victory was equal pay for Negro teachers in 1948. In 1952, he had sued to integrate the New Orleans Public Schools in *Bush v. Orleans Parish School Board*. That suit bounced around the courts until it was reheard and then subsumed by the *Brown* decision. Tureaud was respected in both the white and Negro communities, and while he was not exactly considered an equal by whites at that time, he had enormous courage and a sharp mind and carried himself with great dignity. His white peers in the law respected his demeanor but stopped short of considering him an equal.

Although the Supreme Court's *Brown* decision ordered the public schools of Topeka, Kansas, to integrate with all deliberate speed, the court did not automatically mandate the same order for public schools throughout the country. In each Southern state, the laws of separate but

*Martin with Dutch and my father in discussion with Edgar Taplin and an uniden-
tified student in New Orleans, circa 1955*
C. C. HAYDEL JR., PHOTOGRAPHER

equal had to be individually challenged. So the long line of court battles began.

The Legal Defense and Education Fund Incorporated (often called the INK Fund) of the National Association for the Advancement of Colored People (NAACP) had successfully argued the *Brown* case and was now prepared to assist local attorneys in arguing cases in each state. The INK Fund attorneys included future Supreme Court justice Thurgood Marshall, future federal judges Constance Baker Motley and Robert Carter, and Jack Greenberg, who became a noted law professor. They and other legal greats often came to New Orleans to collaborate with Tureaud on strategy. Dutch, at age twenty-six, was privileged to be part of this team of legal giants. Together, they were forming a strategy to challenge Louisiana segregation laws. And they had optimism that they could do it because now they had federal law on their side.

The team met for the most part in the Claver Building, taking breaks for lunch and, on days when it worked late, dinner. Since these meetings included both black and white attorneys, having meals out posed an obstacle: under Louisiana law, mixed-race groups were not permitted to eat together. The INK Fund attorneys and their cohorts, however, knew they could go to the Dooky Chase restaurant a few blocks down Orleans Avenue, where there was a separate room upstairs, a safe place where the attorneys—and any other mixed-race group—could meet without harassment. The strategizing that went on there, over bowls of Leah Chase's hot gumbo and red beans and rice, helped to undercut the legal foundations of Jim Crow. The restaurant became a landmark of the Civil Rights Movement.

I did not seek a teaching position in the New Orleans Public Schools in 1956 because our first child was due the following February. I did pursue Louisiana teacher certification, only to discover that I did not have all the credentials I needed—even though I had a master's degree and four years of teaching experience! According to the rules, I lacked nine semester hours—three each in Louisiana history, psychology, and science. Dillard University offered all three courses in the fall semester, and since I was free, I decided to take them and complete my teacher certification.

By the end of January 1957, I was late in my pregnancy, and one of my professors was nervous about my looming due date.

"Would you like to take the exam early?" he asked.

"I'll be fine," I said. "I have three more weeks to go."

This didn't quell his anxiety, so I agreed to take the exam two days early. Our daughter, Julie, didn't appear for two more weeks.

I was now eligible for Louisiana teacher certification, but I did not take a teaching position for three more years because Marc, our second child, was born a year later.

We were now living in Pontchartrain Park, one of the biggest and most well-appointed Negro developments ever undertaken in the South. Over a thousand two- and three-bedroom homes sat on lots spacious enough to have backyards where children could play. The park was developed by private investors to provide home ownership to middle-income Negroes; it contained various amenities including a golf course, playgrounds, tennis courts, and a small sports stadium. A campus of Southern University was situated within the development. The park was a conundrum of sorts. While it provided quality housing for Negroes, it was also a step back into Jim Crow restraints. New Orleans historically had been an integrated city in terms of housing; Pontchartrain Park kept the races separate.

I was at home with our children during the day, but I couldn't wait for Dutch to arrive at night and share the happenings on the civil rights legal front. He was now a real part of the change we had returned home to experience. Though I was impatient, I realized that in due time I would be part of that change as well.

Television was coming into its own as a medium; for the first time, people could see the news as it happened. The new medium helped spread civil rights activities; the successes as well as the horrific defeats could be openly seen. The reportage gave Negroes the courage to continue working toward freedom and let the rest of the nation know that we would no longer be silent and submissive.

Meanwhile, my life was filled with the day-to-day triumphs and calamities of being a young mother. This was before diaper services and well before clothes dryers, and I had two toddlers. Though he was always running, Dutch did cook on occasion. Still, I had my hands full.

While I may have been outside the earthmoving events of racial liberation, I still had to confront discrimination. By the end of the 1950s, there were a number of Negro physicians with general practices within New Orleans. Negro surgeons and a few specialists could be found as well, but for some medical specialties, there were no Negro practitioners. Still, some white specialists collaborated with Negro physicians and even treated Negro patients.

In the summer of 1959, I needed to see a dermatologist, and my father recommended a Caucasian physician to whom he had referred other patients. I made an appointment. When I arrived at the doctor's office, I went to the reception desk. It was situated in a large, airy waiting room furnished with upholstered chairs, multiple lamps, lush plants, and a magazine rack. Soft music played in the background. After speaking to the receptionist, I was not allowed to sit in that area but was immediately escorted down the hall to another room. The room was small and square and offered a half-dozen folding chairs and an end table. It had one lamp and a small, high window—no magazines, no upholstered chairs, no music, no plants.

I waited in the colored waiting room for what seemed a very long time. Because I was isolated, I could not see how many white patients were seen before me. Eventually, another Negro patient was brought into the waiting room. Finally, I was called, and the doctor saw me.

I returned for several follow-up visits. Each time, the ritual was the same.

On the sixth visit, I waited for more than two hours to see the doctor. I assumed that if the doctor had an emergency, the staff would have informed me. I became impatient and agitated. I determined that I would never come back again. But I also thought about my father's professional relationship with this doctor. His willingness to see Negro patients was unusual in the South, even in Louisiana. He had a kindly manner and treated me—when I finally saw him—well.

After he saw me, he told me to come back in three weeks. I asked if I could have a word with him. He invited me into his office and offered me a chair.

I hesitated for a second. "This is my last visit," I said.

"Are you leaving town?" he asked.

"No," I said, struggling for what to say next. "I'm not coming back because I won't sit in that room one more time."

"I'm sorry," he said. "I had to set up the separate waiting rooms. It's the law."

"That doesn't make it any easier."

He paused and turned his chair away from me. He now faced a tall window, through which he could view the garden outside. He stayed that way for at least two minutes, just staring. Finally, he turned to me. "I hope things will be different someday," he said.

I said goodbye as politely as I could and went out the door.

I still think about that doctor and others such as the dean at Tulane, who, against their own moral sensibilities, were forced to treat people in such demeaning ways.

That same year, I made my debut in community service and the Civil Rights Movement by joining the women's auxiliary of the Urban League, the Urban League Guild. It was a small thing, but it was what I could do at the time. It was a beginning.

> *We may not get everything we fight for, but we will certainly have to fight for everything we get.*
>
> Frederick Douglass

CHAPTER 9

Negotiation New Orleans-Style

Louisiana's racial issues were no less serious and violent than those in the rest of the South. Still, Louisiana had its own distinctive history, especially in New Orleans and Baton Rouge, and its own way of dealing with racial issues. The lines between the races were blurred here. Because of the peculiar evolution of slavery in the state, many people were, and are, of mixed ancestry. Slave women typically—and most often unwillingly—had children by their masters, and as slavery continued, "black" slaves became increasingly "white." People shared close quarters even while being segregated socially. In a few significant ways, they learned to interact, to exchange goods and services, to survive.

Even during slavery, New Orleans was home to a large community of free people of color, the *gens de colour libre*, some of whom had never been slaves. It had a large population of artisans—bricklayers, carpenters, plasterers, and other skilled construction workers—who did much of the building work in the city. New Orleans also became a haven for newly freed slaves as Jim Crow took effect in the 1890s. A century earlier many Haitians had come to Louisiana after the revolution led by Toussaint L'Ouverture. A class of free people of color became early civil rights activists. They printed a newspaper and formed the protagonists in the *Plessy v. Ferguson* separate-but-equal challenge in the Supreme Court in 1896. In many instances, including the landmark *Plessy* case, Louisiana initiated important changes in civil rights thinking and activism. The significance of these events was often obscured historically because of the unusual, often subtle, way in which they developed. Again, that is not to say that Louisiana did not have its share of racial violence. It did, especially in certain parishes (counties). In the 1960s, Bogalusa, Louisiana, was thought to have the highest per capita Ku Klux Klan membership in America. Plaquemines, southeast of New Orleans, was also a hotbed of racist provocation.

In certain parts of the state, however, overt violence was tempered because of the tradition of compromise that had developed between the races over the centuries. Two years before the Montgomery Bus Boycott, a Baptist minister, T. J. Jemison, had led a bus boycott in Baton Rouge, the Louisiana capital. While the 1956–57 Montgomery boycott led by Martin Luther King lasted thirteen months and was violent, the dispute in Baton Rouge was settled more quickly and quietly. After eight days, through negotiation and compromise with the city council, the old rules, which had left Negro patrons standing while ten assigned "white seats" were vacant, ended. That boycott was the first such action of the Civil Rights Movement in Louisiana and doubtless helped to catalyze what happened in Montgomery. Many south Louisiana residents, white and black, were accustomed to accommodation in a way not yet acceptable in other parts of the South.

Other segregation disputes in Louisiana were similarly resolved. Public libraries in New Orleans were desegregated a year following the bus boycott in Baton Rouge. Rosa Keller, the first Caucasian woman appointed to the library board, asked why Negro children were unable to use the library branch in their own neighborhood. Keller was from a prominent New Orleans family. With her aristocratic bearing and

Southern charm, she went to the mayor, Chep Morrison, and made her plea. He didn't respond immediately, but Keller was a patient woman. Eventually, she got a call one night from Mayor Morrison. He told her that all of the New Orleans public libraries were now open to all citizens. Without any media or other fanfare, the libraries were integrated; the chairs were simply removed from the tables. Drinking fountains and restrooms remained segregated for a short time.

Dutch came home one spring evening in 1958 and told me that the state law requiring segregation on public transportation, which had been challenged years ago, had finally been overturned by United States judge J. Skelly Wright. It was decided by a biracial group of leaders in concert with the transit authority. The signs saying "For Colored Patrons Only" would be removed at midnight, and no media would be alerted. Dutch and I laughed when he told me that some whites had asked that, if desegregation took place without media attention, how Negroes would know they were free to sit anywhere on the buses and streetcars. Those individuals had been assured that the word would be quietly disseminated through our networks, and that people would begin to move freely on the buses. And of course, they did, although haltingly at first.

Aware of the horrific reaction by police in Birmingham to efforts to desegregate, white establishment leaders—bankers, professionals, businessmen, and even Mardi Gras "royalty," a socially and economically elite class—understood what could occur in New Orleans if demonstrations escalated here. They knew violence could damage the city's economy, especially the tourism industry, upon which New Orleans relied so heavily.

Yet the combined forces of the Civil Rights Movement in New Orleans were obviously not going to stand down from a confrontation. The NAACP and the Urban League represented the old guard of the Civil Rights Movement; during the 1960s, they would be joined by the nonviolent Southern Christian Leadership Conference (SCLC), headquartered in Atlanta; the more militant Congress for Racial Equality (CORE); the Student Nonviolent Coordinating Committee (SNCC), which would become progressively more militant; and the Consumers' League, which focused on local economic issues.

Two business districts were targeted for challenges to discriminatory access and hiring practices: Dryades Street, where most of the customers of retail stores were Negro (although the store owners were white), and Canal Street, the main shopping district, where stores and dining facilities denied Negroes access. Dryades Street proved somewhat amenable to traditional tactics such as boycotts and picketing by CORE, which had many students in its ranks. Members of the chamber of commerce and the newly formed Citizens Committee convinced businessmen that integration was inevitable. Soon, hiring practices changed. But sit-ins were necessary to bring attention to segregated lunch counters at Grants, Woolworth's, and McCrory's on Canal Street, and sometimes the stores' responses were ugly. There were many arrests, but the action was effective.

As one of the young attorneys in the movement, Dutch was often asked by parents to convince their college-age children not to demonstrate, but he told them that young people were part of the struggle, and he didn't want them to quit. He did promise that he would try to get their children out of jail if they were arrested and to get their charges expunged. He kept that promise, shuttling back and forth to rescue jailed demonstrators and working to keep their records clean.

In 1960, the United States Supreme Court rendered a decision outlawing segregation in interstate transportation facilities, including terminals. The following year, CORE tested the law by organizing bus rides throughout the South with its younger members, both black and white, and other volunteers from around the country.

These "Freedom Riders" planned to start in Washington, D.C., making stops in various Southern cities and ending in New Orleans. In each Southern city, they tried to use the facilities in the bus stations—the waiting rooms, counters, and restrooms. In many cities, they didn't get that far. They were immediately met by club-wielding local police or attacked by angry mobs sometimes swinging baseball bats and iron pipes. Because they were engaged in a nonviolent protest, the Freedom Riders had to endure the beatings without fighting back. An even worse fate met them in Anniston, Alabama, when their bus was firebombed. Several were wounded and had to be hospitalized. Those who were not seriously injured, as well as new Freedom Rider replacements, continued on another bus. In Jackson, Mississippi, they were again arrested and kept for days.

Although CORE members were waiting for them in New Orleans, they needed to find a place to stay so they could clean up and get some sleep. Rudy Lombard, then a student leader at Xavier University, had an idea. He knew the dorms at Xavier, a Negro university, were empty. The semester was over, and the students had gone home. He asked Norman Francis, then executive vice president at Xavier, if the Freedom Riders could stay in the dorms. Francis knew that law enforcement was waiting to prevent them from demonstrating in the New Orleans bus terminal. It was a risk for Xavier to house the students, but Francis gave his permission. The Freedom Riders arrived the following day. They were bloodied, dirty, and exhausted, but they found a warm, safe haven at Xavier. Law-enforcement officers who were expecting them to turn up in the New Orleans bus station were stymied. The Freedom Riders had seemingly disappeared.

⚜

In 1957, President Eisenhower had sent federal troops (the 101st Airborne Division) into Little Rock to enforce school desegregation. Three years later, in March 1960, Judge Skelly Wright ordered the New Orleans Public Schools to desegregate. The New Orleans establishment did not want the ugliness of Little Rock to be repeated in its city. By then, though, militant White Citizens' Councils had formed to turn back desegregation. Their methods, particularly in Deep South areas, were routinely violent.

In the Louisiana legislature, where rural Louisianans had clout, resistance to integration was also hardcore, and the rhetoric was growing more outrageous. New Orleans could do as it pleased with its businesses, restaurants, and public places, but Governor Jimmy Davis, whose master's thesis had focused on the natural superiority of the Caucasian intellect, decided to draw the line in New Orleans over the schools. He and his supporters didn't care what the New Orleans School Board thought.

In November, four little Negro girls enrolled in formerly all-white schools—three at one school and one at another. In one of the uglier confrontations of the Civil Rights Movement, six-year-old Ruby Bridges faced a crowd of screaming, shouting white protestors. If the obscene language, the spitting, and the crushing mob were not enough to scare her to death, some evil protestors displayed a black doll in a coffin. John Steinbeck, who had documented the miseries of the Great Depression

Federal marshals escorted Ruby Bridges to and from school. As white parents pulled their children from classes, she was soon alone with her teacher. She was frightened but continued to pray for the often-violent protesters: "Forgive them. They don't know what they're doing."
U. S. DEPARTMENT OF JUSTICE

in his epic novel *The Grapes of Wrath*, called the scene of hysterical white women a "witches' Sabbath."

Before long, white families abandoned the first integrated school. One white family remained at the second school but was harassed horribly. The father lost his job, and the family was forced to flee. Meanwhile, the little girls continued their education in isolation. Integration would not move forward for another few years, although the Catholic schools in New Orleans integrated a year later.

I returned to teaching that same year. After my experience in Newton, Massachusetts, among mostly white middle-class families and in Baltimore, Maryland, where I took part in integrating the faculty, I wasn't sure what to expect in the New Orleans Public Schools.

I was assigned to first grade at Henderson Dunn School in the Desire Housing Project. All of us—principal, teachers, staff, and students—were black. Desire, the largest public housing development in New Orleans both in population and size, was located in an isolated area surrounded by railroad tracks and a canal. Many traditional families—father, mother, and children—resided there, as well as families headed by single mothers. Many lived below the poverty level, holding menial jobs. Some were on welfare. There was crime in the area, but we teachers never felt threatened because we were known by the residents. The school was just fifteen minutes from my home.

Teaching at Dunn School was rewarding because the children were eager to learn. They responded to attention and praise and prospered in a structured environment. Some students were challenging, but what school doesn't have a few of those?

While the case for integrating the New Orleans Public Schools was being successfully argued, the Louisiana legislature was busy passing a spate of anti-integration laws that would nullify, or at least delay, the enforcement of the court decision. One such Louisiana law, resurrected from 1924, was actually intended to curtail the activities of the Ku Klux

Klan at that time. The law required certain organizations to register their membership lists with the state. The updated law prohibited anyone from advocating integration or from being a member of an organization that advocated integration.

One of the organizations targeted was the NAACP, whose members included many teachers and principals. The Orleans Parish School Board fell in line with the law and, under threat of dismissal, prohibited its teachers from promoting integration or belonging to organizations promoting integration. I was still teaching at Dunn School, a New Orleans public school, at that point. By then, I belonged to several civil rights organizations that promoted integration, including the NAACP and the Urban League.

One evening after dinner, Dutch was bringing me up to date on the events of the day. He mentioned that teachers were unwilling to get out front to challenge the law, fearing dismissal. I could see from the look on his face that he was turning something over in his brain.

"You could be the plaintiff," he said, "but we can't afford to lose your salary."

"You're right. We can't. What teacher could afford that?"

He looked resigned, but I was unwilling to let the chance pass.

"Let me see if I can do some creative budgeting," I said.

By the time he came home the next day, I had worked up some numbers. I told him, "We can manage, but only if it doesn't take a long time to get a ruling in our favor."

Dutch smiled. "I will prepare a brief and file it tomorrow."

Each day for the next month, I went off to school expecting the ax to fall, expecting to be dismissed. I waited and waited, but nothing happened. Finally, Dutch called just as I got home from work one day.

"Sybil, listen to this," he said. "We've won our case—by default."

"What do you mean?"

"I'll explain when I get home."

When he arrived, Dutch told me what had happened. It turned out that our case did not come to trial. Rather, the law proved unenforceable. In fact, all the Jim Crow laws became unenforceable as the federal courts overruled state courts across the South. I kept my membership in the NAACP and the Urban League and continued teaching.

⚜

One by one in Louisiana and throughout the South, laws enacted to safeguard segregation and punish its opponents were challenged successfully. Not only did this open doors for Negroes, but the dismantling of such laws dissuaded legislatures from trying to pass new Jim Crow legislation.

Dutch and I had five children within a span of thirteen years, so there was at least one baby at home for many years. Throughout my teaching career, we employed a nanny/housekeeper to care for the children until I got home from work at four o'clock. When I had to attend meetings, I found high-school and college students in the neighborhood who were competent sitters. They would look after the children until they were ready for bed. One student, Judy Lopez, who eventually became an elementary-school teacher, began sitting with our children when she was in high school and continued through college. Years later, she worked as a wonderful tutor and sitter with my grandchildren.

In the mid-sixties, I requested an uptown teaching assignment so I could drive Julie to school at Ursuline Academy. I began teaching at Mc-Donogh #24 School in a nearby neighborhood known as "Black Pearl" or "Niggertown," depending upon who was naming it. The families lived in rentals and were generally poor, but they resided near the grand houses on stately St. Charles Avenue. The children had access to a diverse environment and were more streetwise than the children in Desire. Very soon, I would get a personal look at that "streetwise disposition" in the person of one of my more colorful students.

> *It is a peculiar sensation, this double-consciousness, this sense of always looking at oneself through the eyes of others, of measuring one's soul by the tape of a world that looks on in amused contempt and pity.*
>
> W. E. B. Du Bois

CHAPTER 10

Cultural Deprivation

Nine-year-old Jessie Mae was a complete busybody—always the center of attention. This early morning was no different. When she came into my third-grade classroom, she was sweaty and covered with dirt, as though she had been rolling on the ground. Her hair had become unbraided and was standing straight up. Tears rolled down her dusty cheeks. In a loud voice, she announced that Billy, a classmate, had beaten her up on the way to school.

Given her history, I was more than a little suspicious. I wondered if she had actually started the fight.

"And just why did Billy beat you up, Jessie Mae?"

"He called me black, and I punched him in the nose. Because nobody is going to call me black and get away with it."

"And what is wrong with being black?" I asked.

I remember that moment well; somewhere inside me, something came to a standstill. My own childhood, my own psychological drama, was playing out before my eyes. For I, as well as many white people, believed that *black* was a derogatory word to describe my people. Suddenly,

I realized that I, too, was a victim of the white-imposed concept of my race. Since our ancestors had been kidnapped from Africa and sold into slavery and eventually emancipated, we had been brainwashed to believe that our black skin, kinky hair, and broad facial features were ugly. To be called *black* by one of our own—another Negro—was a fighting provocation.

A light went on in my head. This time, I almost shouted: "What is the matter with being black?"

Jessie Mae stared up at me, looking somewhat perplexed, and I realized I needed to talk to her later in private. But first, I needed some information. I settled the class with an independent writing assignment and called Billy up to my desk.

"Billy, did you call Jessie Mae black?"

"Yeah, 'cause she is always messin' with me."

"Just how does she do that?"

"She comes close to me and pushes me. She calls me stupid and runs off. She's a bully."

"Did you think calling her black was the same as her calling you stupid?"

"I knew it would make her really mad," he replied, looking rather sheepish.

"Calling a Negro black shouldn't start a fight. What's wrong with being black? Black is not ugly; black is beautiful. We shouldn't hate the way we look. We should see the beauty in our looks. We look the way God wants us to look."

After that incident, I led informal discussions with the class; we talked about black characteristics and my students' thoughts about how they looked.

I left that school the next year and returned to Dunn School. I don't know what kind of adult Jessie Mae became, but I suspect, with her spunk, she may have made something of herself.

The "Black Is Beautiful" consciousness going on at that time invaded my psyche. It was heady and freed me, as well as thousands of other Negroes, from self-denigration. We became more aware and accepting of our African physical characteristics and learned how to be proud of our skin, hair, and facial features. The Caucasian standard of beauty—blond hair, blue eyes, and fair skin—was no longer the only one of value. We didn't look like that; we couldn't look like that. Our acceptance of that standard was part of our race's continued enslavement. Our eventual rejection of it became part of our liberation. We began to wear colorful African clothing and adopted hairstyles, including Afros and cornrows, that were natural expressions of our culture. Some clothes—and even hairstyles—would eventually be emulated by Caucasians.

The issue of standards of beauty, in fact, had come up during arguments in *Brown v. Board of Education* and even played a role in the decision. Prominent black psychologist Kenneth Clark and his wife, Mamie, presented dolls of different races to determine which doll Negro girls liked best. In the majority of cases, they chose the white doll. They viewed white dolls as "pretty" and "good" and black dolls as "ugly" and "bad." The conclusion was that Negro children were conditioned to think less of their own physical attributes than those of Caucasians. The Clarks testified in several desegregation cases, including *Brown*. The results of their testing helped undermine the foundation of the separate-but-equal principle.

In Louisiana, skin color had always constituted a sideshow in terms of social relations, both within the Negro community and between blacks and whites. A kind of caste system, sometimes quite extreme and bizarre, grew out of the labeling of blood percentages. People were labeled quadroons, octoroons, etc. The percentage of white blood gave one privilege in society, so it helped further degrade black skin color and black identity.

However, skin color and physical attributes were not the only things that slavery and its aftermath degraded. The entire diverse and accomplished culture of Negroes was disparaged. The term *culturally deprived* came into common usage during and after the Civil Rights Movement. It was used to describe blacks entering the mainstream who, because of segregation and discrimination, had limited or no exposure to the majority society. *Separate* had never meant *equal*, and Negroes did not have access to the academic and social resources that whites did. Jim Crow laws and contemporary mores shut them out of the mainstream.

Because of the separation of the races, neither knew much about how the other half lived. Although many New Orleans neighborhoods were integrated before 1950, black people nevertheless stayed mostly isolated. The races socialized, shopped, and worshiped in different places. Blacks had little contact with white people; what contact existed was superficial, and generally in the context of employment. Many black people worked in white homes and businesses, but they remained in subservient positions that offered limited conversation and social interaction. As a result, all blacks excepting the servant class knew very little about white people and how they lived.

Whites suffered a cultural deprivation of their own. The blacks they came in contact with in most cases were not peers or colleagues. Except for the servant class, black people were not a part of their lives. As the dominant race, whites had no reason to learn about Negroes and, possibly, little interest in doing so. In New Orleans, this was particularly odd because many of our traditional neighborhoods were mixed. I played with both black and white children when I was young, but we went off to separate schools, parks, playgrounds, and churches. Gradually, the ties we had as young children disappeared.

⚜

In the 1960s, when urban planners realized that playgrounds and swimming pools would be open to Negroes, they quickly erected a number of new playgrounds and swimming pools in Negro neighborhoods. The Olympic-sized pool at Audubon Park was closed permanently to skirt the mandate that would eventually come down from the court integrating the pools.

The court decisions at the state level and two sweeping congressional acts—the Civil Rights Act (Public Accommodations Act) in 1964 and the Voting Rights Act in 1965—opened the doors in the public sector and gave blacks a voice at the polls. New Orleans also achieved some changes through negotiations, rather than legislation.

As cases asserting equal rights were successfully tried and the knot of segregation began to loosen, blacks of all economic strata found themselves able to enter some doors that had been previously locked. It wasn't always easy, because we had been excluded from social, educational, and employment opportunities and now had to play catch-up to compete with a majority population not generally eager to embrace us. Black people had to discover how to achieve success in the mainstream, had to learn what it took to excel in once white-only schools and jobs, as well as which avocations to pursue to expand our skills, intellectual interests, and contacts.

There was a steep learning curve, and the playing field was not always level. On the other hand, New Orleans for decades had nurtured a distinct black professional class. My father and another black man on our block were practicing physicians. The Creole culture in New Orleans and Louisiana was manifested in large numbers of gifted artists, artisans, craftsmen, and musicians. Louisiana had its black servant class, of course, but it also had a black middle class and upper middle class.

Many black people had the same pioneering spirit as the groups of immigrants who had come willingly to America. But blacks had been operating, and would continue to operate, under the adversity of second-class citizenship. This gave us a peculiar strength that, if others took the time to notice, taught a truly American lesson. Blacks, toughened by the very conditions that enslaved and then restricted us, learned how to be strong in the face of adversity. We learned how to cope in a hostile environment and not become bitter or despairing. We were pioneers not so much in the geographical sense but in the realm of courage.

But to many whites, we were, and continued to be, all but invisible. To see us, to actually recognize us, required the admission that a whole pattern of behavior, the history of several centuries, was a moral error of enormous proportions.

Dutch and I had white friends who were sympathetic to the idea of an America that was fair and just to all citizens. They were people of conscience who chose to publicly assert their beliefs. Among them were white members of the Urban League, academics from the local universities, people from various Christian churches, Jewish people who knew what discrimination and rejection felt like, and some social and economic elites who made the choice to act on their principles. Now, with all the legal barriers down, other white people stepped forward to befriend black people.

One couple, Clare and Harold Katner, whose children attended the same school my children did, invited my family to dinner, and we and our children became friends. Claire told me months later that one of her neighbors admonished her own children to "be nice to the colored children, but don't play with them." Some whites who might have befriended us didn't because they feared ostracism from their friends.

Two white federal judges played important roles in the struggle for justice and equality, ruling consistently on the many cases that reversed the separate-but-equal laws in the state, including the racist laws enacted by the Louisiana legislature in the early 1960s. The two judges came from very different backgrounds.

A New Orleans native, Judge J. Skelly Wright of the United States District Court was a Catholic from a working-class family and neighborhood. He graduated from public school and Loyola University Law

School. It was Skelly Wright who ordered the admission of blacks to Louisiana State University Law School in 1952. He later wrote that "ordering LSU Law School integrated was my first integration order. Until that time, I was just another Southern 'boy.' After it, there was no turning back."

Judge John Minor Wisdom of the United States Court of Appeals, Fifth District, came from a prominent family in New Orleans. He also had a fundamental commitment to the rule of law, the United States Constitution, and the decisions of the Supreme Court.

Changes in the law brought about by free-thinking judges such as Wright and Wisdom, and later Judge Herbert Christenberry, helped to improve people's conditions and consciousness. In New Orleans as well as the nation, such jurists were changing the idea of justice.

CHAPTER 11

Into the Trenches

"Did you see the news today? Did you see the way they beat our people back for wanting our rights as American citizens? Did you see the meanness and anger in their faces? You know, that could be you or me or your children or grandchildren. If we want our rights, we have to vote for our rights. We have to elect people who respect us. I have my say when I vote. We need all of you to do the same."

We were opening one of our Louisiana League of Good Government (LLOGG) voter registration workshops. Frank, one of the first residents of the Guste Homes Senior Citizens Apartments, was one of our best cheerleaders for voter registration. He was a distinguished, wellspoken gentleman who always wore a suit to our meetings. He was already a registered voter but came to our workshops almost every week. His wife, a soft-spoken, gentle woman, often accompanied him. Frank became a major spokesperson for the voting effort. He would start off by challenging the residents to make the effort to register and often ended up accompanying them to the registrar's office, encouraging them and putting them at ease. At the start of a workshop, he would ask who had registered, urging them to stand while everyone applauded.

On the surface, it seemed easy enough—registering to vote. However, for nearly a hundred years in the South, voting rights had been clenched in the hands of white politicians loath to lose their sovereignty in elections. Still, if Negroes were to gain even a foothold in the realm of political power, we had to vote. There was no other way. Yet, as I had discovered earlier, little underpinning existed for such a struggle.

In 1961, I learned about the League of Women Voters from a friend from New York. We talked about some of its activities, especially its work in voter registration. We had a conversation about voting as one of the major vehicles for overcoming inequality. She said she would put my name up for membership. Soon, however, we learned that, because of state laws, the league was not open to Negro women in Louisiana. That shut door was an epiphany for me. I decided that this was where I— along with my friends—could contribute to the Civil Rights Movement. We should form our own organization and work to get our own people registered to vote. Other organizations were involved in voter registration, including the local NAACP, but ours would start from our home ground, where we stood, and grow from there. The more people involved in the effort, I thought, the more voters we could harvest.

I brought up the idea informally to a group of friends involved in community activities. We were named CiCulSo, an acronym for Civic, Cultural, and Social Organization. We were all young mothers. Seven of us—Judy Arnaud, Barbara Clanton, Lillian Jones, Gladys Jordan, Louadrian Reed, Charmaine Young, and I—also worked outside the home and were involved with charitable groups. At one of our early get-togethers, we agreed that we were benched on the sidelines while the Civil Rights Movement was playing out in front of our eyes. I related my rejection for membership in the League of Women Voters and proposed that there were two things we could do: help our people to become registered voters and educate ourselves on the workings of government. In this way, we could become enlightened voters and share our knowledge with others. We were all enthusiastic. Here was a way we could make a real contribution. Our own communities, where we once had felt politically confined, could become our base of activity in preparing potential voters and offering guidance about making informed choices.

In the beginning, we met at my home and the homes of other members. Quickly, we established our purpose and selected a name. An all-female group at the time, we incorporated in 1963 with the following mandate: "The Louisiana League of Good Government is a non-partisan, integrated"—at the time, we had one white member—"women's organization whose purpose is to promote good government through an informed and participating citizenry."

We got to work immediately and quickly expanded our group, inviting other women we thought might be interested. At our initial meeting, held in the auditorium of the historic Claver Building, we had sixty-five women in attendance. I was elected president.

Our first project was to become familiar with the voter registration process and all the impediments that kept down the number of Negro voters. These impediments were formidable and sometimes unpredictable. The stated registration process required passing a literacy test and a citizenship test; computing one's age in years, months, and days; and providing "correct" identification. Such identification could change at the whim of a deputy registrar and might include a driver's license, a social security card, a utility or water bill, and/or a rent lease.

We selected three heavily Negro-populated areas to hold voter registration workshops—two in welcoming churches and one in a senior citizens' center. One night a week, a committee of three LLOGG women went to one of the sites to conduct the information sessions. The people were enthusiastic about the possibility of becoming registered voters and were willing learners. We tutored them on the literacy and citizenship test requirements and alerted them to the potentially hostile responses they might encounter.

At the Guste Homes Senior Citizens Center—the first in the city for black seniors, built by the United States Department of Housing and Urban Development—LLOGG held voter registration workshops every Tuesday night. Most of the attendees were senior citizens and residents. As word got around about our efforts, people from the neighboring housing developments also joined our workshops.

Clara was one attendee who I would guess was in her late seventies or early eighties. She was short, slim, and spry. I learned her story over a series of conversations. She had grown up in rural southwestern Louisiana in Church Point and lived there for many years, raising her seven children, most of whom continued to live in that area. She was widowed and wished she could be near her grandchildren, but she liked living on her own in New Orleans at the Guste Homes, where she had friends her own age.

The first day I met her, she said, "I have wanted to be able to vote as long as I can remember. My mama used to tell us stories about slavery days and about the lynchings of our people. I thought that was so awful and wished I could vote so maybe I could help stop the way our people were treated."

Clara was very serious about preparing to register to vote. I went over the information with a small group and then worked with her individually. After a few sessions, I said, "Clara, I think you are ready for the test! Let's go over the material one more time." She was so excited.

Along with three other residents, she rode in the Guste Homes van to the registrar of voters' office.

When I arrived at the Guste Homes for the workshop the following week, Clara came up to me with an unhappy look: "Mrs. Morial, I didn't make it. I was so nervous, I think I had some of the test answers wrong.

But I want to study more and try again."

We went over the material again that night, and I told her to review it during the week. She was confident that she was prepared and anxious to try again, but when I saw her at the next workshop, she was sad and aggravated. She told me the registrar had rattled her; he rushed her on the literacy test, during which she had to read the Preamble to the United States Constitution. She missed some words and failed.

"But I'm not giving up, Mrs. Morial. I am going again, and I will make it this time!"

We reviewed again, and I knew she was ready. I told her I would go with her.

We had a school holiday that day, so I went to pick her up, along with two others. Before we left for the registrar's office, I asked them all, "Do you have the proper identification?"

They all answered in unison: "Yes!"

"We all brought more than we need," Clara said.

They went into the office, and I waited outside near the door. A little while later, Clara came out, once again in tears. This time, she was inconsolable. I tried to hug her.

"That mean man was so ugly to me. He told me I wasn't smart enough to vote. I know I had the right identification, I read the Preamble without any mistakes, and I passed that citizenship test. My age in years, months, and days was right, because you helped me figure it out. Mrs. Morial, will I ever be able to vote?"

I didn't say so, but I began to wonder myself if Clara would ever be able to get through the obstacles thrown at her. It would have been easy to give up, especially considering her years. The odds seemed stacked against her, but Clara went back a fourth time. Again, she came out with tears streaming down her face. But as she got closer, I saw that these were tears of another kind.

She grabbed me and hugged me. "I made it, Mrs. Morial. I can vote! Praise the Lord!"

Some had to return several times, and some were humiliated. Watching others' eventual success, however, very few stayed discouraged. Voting had been a dream for a long time; they would not forsake that dream. The LLOGG project went on for three years until the Voting Rights Act was passed in 1965. At that point, all the complicated requirements for voter registration across the nation were struck down.

Our second major project was educating people about the political process. We began with ourselves and then shared the knowledge with others. A judge came to one of our education meetings to talk about the judicial system and all the various courts and their jurisdictions. Another guest was a city councilman, who talked about the responsibilities and duties of the city council. One topic I found especially interesting was the state legislature and its workings, and how we could lend our voices to various bills that were being considered. We had no idea what a bond issue was, so a guest was invited to talk about that. By and by, our members

Reverend Martin Luther King Jr. and supporters witness President Lyndon Johnson signing the Voting Rights Act. What we had long fought for was now a reality.
WHITE HOUSE PHOTO

were becoming informed. We told our people, "Now you can vote. Now do it!"

We expanded our efforts with Get Out the Vote drives, reminding our people of upcoming elections and making materials about all candidates available. I knew that if we became partisan and recommended or endorsed candidates, we might become divisive.

Up to that time, white candidates had talked to Negro political organizations but had not addressed large groups of voters directly. I asked a friend who was a candidate for the city council, Moon Landrieu, who later became mayor, if he thought white candidates would come speak to our membership. He said he didn't know for certain, but he would be there. On the night of the event, we had such a large turnout of candidates that all of them could not actually speak, though they were all able to work the crowd. That event put us on the map, and for the next thirty-three years, we had a well-attended Meet the Candidates event.

A few months after we organized, we discussed ways to increase our membership. One of our charter members, Barbara Clanton, offered an idea: "Women like to dress up and come to something social. Let's have a membership luncheon."

It was a grand idea, but where could we do it? It was the spring of 1963, and hotels and restaurants were not open to Negroes. It would take another year before the civil rights laws opened public places to us. The few Negro-owned restaurants in New Orleans were not large enough.

I knew that the movie producer Otto Preminger had held a posh luncheon at the Royal Orleans Hotel on the occasion of the world premiere of the movie *The Cardinal*. Negroes were present at the event. Preminger insisted that the city's most important people be there as his guests—and that there be Negroes in attendance. The hotel conceded, and a very few were invited. I thought, *Let's give it a shot. What can they say other than no?*

I made an appointment to see the hotel manager and was told I needed to see the sales manager if I wanted to schedule an event. I kept the appointment. When introduced, I told the sales manager about LLOGG's purpose, and that our organization was integrated (by then, we had a couple of white benefactors and several white members). I told him directly that we wanted to have a luncheon at the hotel. The sales manager said she would get back to me. The next day, she called and said that we were welcome to have our luncheon there.

That was the first hotel to open its doors to Negroes. We made quiet history and earned a reputation as a progressive organization that got things done. We planned on seventy-five guests, but when word got around that the event was at the Royal Orleans Hotel, an elegant, relatively new establishment, the number swelled to almost three hundred women. Our speaker was a member of the League of Women Voters. The event was a smashing success, increased our membership, and swelled the number of women working on our projects.

Each year thereafter, we held a membership luncheon and invited a Negro woman of national prominence as our speaker. Among the speakers were California congresswomen Yvonne Braithwaite Burke and Maxine Waters; federal judge Constance Baker Motley; Ruby Grant Martin from the Office of Civil Rights in the Department of Health, Education, and Welfare; syndicated journalist and economist Julianne Malveaux; and many others, all of whom inspired us to keep going.

⚜

I can no longer remember each poignant moment, each inspiration, in the struggle for the vote and the quest for a voice in our American destiny. Some, though, have proven unforgettable.

Alma was a tall, attractive, and confident woman. She came to LLOGG's first voter registration workshop at the Guste Homes and announced that she had always wanted to become a registered voter. Still, she had heard repeatedly how badly Negroes were treated when they went to register. She shook her head and continued, "I was scared. But after I heard about the bombing of that Birmingham church where those four little girls, the same age as my grandchildren, were killed, I was so upset and angry that anyone could do that. I decided I would become a voter no matter what, no matter how they treated me."

She proved a serious learner. Alma took the materials home to study, came to the next workshop a week later, and said, "I'm ready! I want to register tomorrow."

And in fact, she did go to the registrar of voters' office the very next day. A week later, she waltzed into the workshop singing, "I can vote, I can vote, I can say my piece in the voting booth!"

Alma became a recruiter in the Guste Homes, in the surrounding housing developments, and at her church, telling everyone about becoming registered. At the workshop after her success, she stood before the group and said, "If I did it, you can, too. Just think about those little girls who died in the church bombing. Just think about those awful policemen beating our people. Just think about them dogs and fire hoses pushing our people back. If that don't make you mad enough to want to vote, well, I feel sorry for you."

After that speech, our attendance grew to such a size that we began doing two workshops per week. We reached out to the residents who lived in the neighboring housing developments and invited them to the workshops. We named Alma as assistant secretary. Her duties were to take care of the voter materials and help anyone who wanted to study for the literacy test and the citizenship test. She was thrilled with the position and carried out her duties efficiently.

In 1964, a year and a half after LLOGG incorporated, the League of Women Voters invited our organization to merge with it. State laws had changed, and blacks and whites were no longer prohibited from eating or meeting together. We decided to decline because we had a specific agenda that we thought was still needed by the black community.

When Dutch ran for and won a seat in the Louisiana legislature, I resigned as president of LLOGG to ensure that the organization remained nonpartisan. I held no office and kept a low profile, but I was in a position to help with speakers, with activities in the legislature, and with ideas for projects.

LLOGG continued to be active for forty years until Hurricane Katrina stripped it of many of its loyal members, who were forced to relocate or to concentrate on surviving the aftermath of the storm.

You can kill a man. But you can't kill an idea.

Myrlie Evers

CHAPTER 12

A Voice in the Night

In 1961, Dutch was elected president of the New Orleans chapter of the National Association for the Advancement of Colored People. Immediately, he became a public figure.

Most people now associate the development of the NAACP with the Civil Rights Movement of the 1950s and 1960s. However, the organization was established in 1908 in response to the lynching of two black men in Springfield, Illinois. The murders evoked a wide response among white Northerners at the time, particularly in answer to a call by a white woman, Mary W. Ovington. She urged the development of an organization to discuss ways of achieving political and social equality for Negroes and other people of color. A conference led to the formation of the NAACP. Though it seems strange today, the organization was initially headed by seven prominent white Americans and only one black, W. E. B. Du Bois. His selection was radical at the time because Du Bois rejected the policy of gradual acquisition of rights for Negroes. Instead, he insisted upon immediate equality. Du Bois became the editor of the

NAACP's periodical, *The Crisis*, which reported on race relations in the United States and around the world.

During the 1950s, the NAACP in Louisiana had to go underground due to the increasing threats, legal and otherwise, to its work. Members were likely to lose their jobs if their memberships were revealed. The organization operated in that way under another name with a different president until Dutch and I (as plaintiff) challenged the law that prohibited teachers from belonging to any organization that advocated integration. Many members of the NAACP at that time were educators.

The community at large, especially the racist White Citizens' Council groups organized throughout the Deep South, resisted the changes brought on by the challenge to Jim Crow laws. The NAACP was a lightning rod, pushing arguments through the courts and urging citizens to support its efforts.

Under Dutch's leadership, the membership in New Orleans grew. He became the spokesperson in Louisiana for the oldest and what had now become the chief black activist group in the United States. Dutch's visibility and outspokenness made him a principal focus of resistance—and then harassment.

Soon after he became president of the local organization, we began receiving threatening phone calls. One summer evening in 1962, the children were playing in the carport and I was preparing dinner when the phone rang. I picked it up and said hello.

As soon as I heard the voice, I knew something was wrong. It was raspy, ugly.

"Where's that nigger communist?" the male voice demanded. "Put him on the phone so I can tell him what I think of him."

I hung up immediately. My hands were trembling. I felt stung and scared.

Several minutes later, the phone rang again. I hesitated before picking it up, thinking it might be the same caller. But I heard Jean's voice and breathed again. I did not mention the call to her; I didn't want anyone to worry.

Soon, Dutch came home, and I told him about the call. He said I had done the right thing to hang up. In those days, telephone calls were not easily traceable. We had little hope of tracking the caller.

Two days later, about the same time, I received another call. It sounded like the same voice, although this time the man used obscene language along with his racist slurs.

A couple of hours later, the phone rang again, and one of the children answered. It was the same obscene message, and I forbade the children to answer the phone from then on.

Some days later, though, on an evening while Dutch and I were out, the babysitter picked up a threatening call. She was very upset, and it was then that I decided to stay home with the children in case the threats became more explicit or physical.

As the calls escalated, they became more threatening, but the voice sounded the same. I usually hung up quickly. Dutch and I thought that the calls, although scary, might forewarn us and keep us alert, so we didn't consider changing our telephone number.

By 1963, the Civil Rights Movement had taken hold all over the South, and resistance had become extremely violent. We had lived in fear since Dutch assumed the NAACP presidency in New Orleans. But the murder of Medgar Evers emboldened racist terrorists across the South. Evers was field secretary of the NAACP in Mississippi when he was killed in June 1963. Gunned down as he got out of his car in his own driveway, he had crawled, bleeding, to his front door, where his wife found him.

That very day, we received another call at night, still the same terrifying voice as the previous calls: "Morial is going to get what that nigger in Mississippi got."

Now, Dutch's murder seemed a real possibility. I was completely frightened, but Dutch was angry that we had to tolerate these calls. Still, with the children in the house, he knew something had to be done. After they had gone to bed, he came to me and said, "That last call is really a threat. We have to take precautions."

Medgar Evers had trained his children to drop to the floor of their house if shots were fired. On the night he was killed, they did just that, hiding in their bedrooms as their father died. I thought we might have to train our children to do the same. Late into the night, lying in bed, we talked about how to protect them in case anything happened. We resolved that when Dutch came home—usually after dark—he would pull into the carport and blow the horn. I would flash the carport light several times, and Dutch would wait a couple of minutes and then come inside. We thought the car horn and the flashing light might startle anyone lying in wait near the house and thwart an assassination plan.

In the middle of the next night, a call came in, and Dutch answered. Before the raspy voice finished its first sentence, Dutch blasted an unrepeatable retort. The caller hung up.

Although we didn't hear the voice for the next couple of weeks, Dutch was receiving hate mail at the office. Opposition to desegregation kept mounting.

Then the calls to our house resumed, just as menacing: "We are going to round you niggers up, especially you loudmouth communist niggers, and put all of you in the stockade at Fort St. Philip out in the swamp, where the alligators and snakes can teach you a lesson."

That was a pretty good description of the edges of Plaquemines Parish, where fields rich in oil and sulfur were surrounded by tidal swamps. Nearby, a fort built by the French in 1724 and later occupied by the Spanish lay in ruins. If rattlesnakes, water moccasins, and swarms of mosquitoes didn't make the place forbidding enough, there were strings of electrically charged barbed-wire fence riding five feet over the brick walls surrounding the fort.

Those were intimidating threats, but we managed to survive them, and they stopped after Dutch moved to a new position in 1964.

I am here because I want to see with my own eyes what the unhappy alliance of wind and water have done to this land and to its good people.... I have ordered that all red tape be cut.

President Lyndon Johnson in
New Orleans, 1965

CHAPTER 13

Betsy, Then Jean

In 1964, Dutch, as a second-term president of the New Orleans NAACP, was identified as a civil rights attorney and activist. So he was surprised to get a call from the United States attorney for the Eastern District of Louisiana, Louis Lacour. Lacour was an intriguing character. Appointed by JFK in 1962, he had prosecuted a variety of well-publicized cases, including one against black radical H. Rap Brown. He had also negotiated the contested matriculation of James Meredith into the University of Mississippi.

Without telling him the nature of his call, Lacour summoned Dutch to his office. When Dutch arrived, he was greeted warmly. Without any fanfare, Lacour invited Dutch to join his staff as an assistant United States attorney for the Eastern District. My husband, rarely taken aback, was thunderstruck. A Negro attorney had never held that position. Dutch thanked Lacour and asked if he could think about it overnight. Lacour agreed.

We talked about it that night. While Dutch was pleased and flattered, taking the position would remove him from the civil rights struggle directly, as well as end his law practice. He would also have to give up the presidency of the NAACP. It occurred to him that this offer might be a contrived way to get him off the scene, to silence him. The federal position was a full-time one, and when he left it, he would have to start up his law practice again. He had a family to support. He reluctantly decided to decline the offer, but he told Lacour he could recommend another attorney for the position. Lacour responded that he wanted Dutch, and only him. The position was not open to anyone else.

That settled it. Dutch could not refuse this "first" opportunity in the fight for equality, lest it not be given to another Negro attorney. If this was a ploy to get him out of the public eye, that would assuredly backfire. Dutch was in possession of a disposition not easily or long deterred.

He was sworn in the following week. His mentor, A. P. Tureaud, was in attendance, as were our children—Julie, seven; Marc, six; and Jacques, three—and extended family.

Mr. Tureaud sidled up to Jacques and asked him, "Just what is your daddy swearing in to be?"

Jacques responded smartly, "President of the United States." He had recently seen Lyndon Johnson on television being sworn in as president. It didn't occur to him that this was any different.

During the three years that Dutch served as assistant United States attorney, he was out of the limelight. Surprisingly, he was not given the civil rights docket, but rather the admiralty/maritime docket. Cases in the civil rights docket soon changed, partly because President Johnson had signed the 1964 Civil Rights Act. Despite his new role, Dutch never took his eyes off the progress of civil rights and his part in the movement.

⚜

In Louisiana, other threats were looming, although this time they weren't political. Early in September 1965, we learned that Hurricane

Betsy was moving up the coast to the Carolinas. Unexpectedly, it made a complete loop and moved southwest toward southern Florida, sweeping over Miami and into the Gulf of Mexico. Along the way, Betsy strengthened into a Category 4 storm.

Early on September 9, New Orleans citizens were warned by radio and television to get extra food that would not have to be cooked, to store a water supply, to fill their gas tanks, and to prepare flashlights and other emergency light sources. We were also advised to check that our battery-powered radios were fully charged.

I was pregnant with Cheri, who was due in early January. Still, I needed to pick up some things and collect Julie, Marc, and Jacques from school. As they got into the car, rain was beginning to come down hard. The streets were crowded with traffic; people were racing home before the flooding began. When we arrived home, the telephone was ringing. It was Dutch. He had been trying to reach me and was concerned that I was okay. I assured him that the children and I were at home, and that I had shopped for all the necessary supplies. In New Orleans, hurricane scares were regular occurrences. We knew the routine.

Shortly after he called, Dutch left the office, but an hour passed and he didn't arrive. It was a trip that normally took fifteen minutes. I started to worry. When he finally got home an hour late, he was unnerved. He said he sensed a rising panic as he plowed through heavy traffic. There were reports of a large surge in Lake Pontchartrain, the largest lake in the United States outside the Great Lakes. Pontchartrain was less than half a mile from our house.

I called my mother, who lived much farther into town, and asked if we could come over until the storm eased. Of course, she welcomed us. She said my father had just closed his office and was on his way home.

The sky was eerily gray, and the rain was light and continuous. We quickly packed the hurricane supplies and some clothing for the next day. It was coming nightfall when we loaded the children in the car. The streets were flooding, a common occurrence in below-sea-level New Orleans. We made our way slowly through the deepening water.

When we arrived at my parents' house, we parked in the driveway under the portico; as children, Jean and I and our friends had played jacks there among the shrubs and flowers. When the wind began blowing hard again, we moved the cars to the long driveway, away from the large live oak tree. Those giants have wide but shallow roots; the wind tends to get under the canopies and uproot them.

The family was already there, including my mother and father, Jean, and Cookie (Glenn), whom I had doted on as a child. He was now a college student, and I was overjoyed to see him. It was a Friday, and Mother had cooked Creole white beans in anticipation of a rainy weekend. Their aroma, tinged with bacon, spread through the house. Her white beans were the best in the world, with a unique flavor and creaminess. Her secret was to cook them first on top of the stove and then bake them for a time covered with strips of bacon in a very low oven. Whenever she cooked red or white beans, she sent a casserole dish to me, enough to feed my family.

Not long after dinner, we all settled in for some sleep, comforted by warm food and the presence of family. The hurricane, though, was not sleeping. As evening fell, it made landfall in Grand Isle, Louisiana, then made its way north, upriver, lifting the Mississippi at New Orleans by a full ten feet. In the middle of the night, we awoke to a crashing sound. The French doors in the living room had blown in, and shards of wet glass covered the floor. Dutch, Cookie, and Marc all scrambled to find something to hold those doors shut. My father rushed into the garage for something that would cover the doors and hold them closed. He came in with an armful of two-by-fours. As the others strained to hold the boards in place, he nailed them to the doorjambs. By the time they secured the doors, it was dawn; we were wide awake. The power was out, but we used the gas stove to make an early breakfast.

Betsy was in full rage. The young children got scared looks on their faces every time something hit the house. We tried to entertain them; I had packed books and board games, and these offered some distraction.

After a day and a half, the raging wind and rain subsided. There was still no power in most of the city. The heat and the dense humidity were overwhelming. When the dark set in, we sat on the cool tiles of the front porch, where we could catch a refreshing breeze every now and then. Neighbors were out on their stoops; they, too, were trying to lighten the tension left by Betsy.

When the hurricane finally passed, there was an eerie stillness all about. We ventured out in the car, found a Royal Castle hamburger outlet open, and went in for lunch. When the server presented all seven of our hamburgers on bread ends, Dutch told him that was not acceptable.

"These are hard times," the server replied dismissively.

Dutch nodded his head, then said, "One or maybe two bread ends, but not all seven."

When we arrived back at my parents' home, we learned that a levee had broken, drowning the Lower Ninth Ward. Pontchartrain Park, our neighborhood, and others near the lake were being flooded.

We remained at my parents' home for a week, improvising meals on Mother's gas stove and rationing water—and waiting for the floodwaters to recede.

At the insistence of Louisiana senator Russell Long, President Johnson flew into New Orleans the day after Betsy made landfall. The president had just signed the Voting Rights Act in August, and Long convinced him that visiting New Orleans was a political necessity. Although he made public speeches about the disaster, it was his journey to the Lower Ninth Ward, recorded in his presidential diary, that echoes through New Orleans' history. The president got down on the ground and, accompanied by Secret Service men armed with flashlights, toured the flooded neighborhoods. At one point, the president approached a schoolhouse that had been converted into a shelter. He stared into the dim, murky rooms, where he could hear the plaintive voices of adults and the whimpering of children. "This is your president," Johnson called through the darkness. "I am here to help you."

After the waters receded, Dutch and I went to our home to view the damage. The streets in Pontchartrain Park were like canals, not navigable by foot or car. From the edge of the flooding, a friend took us to our house in a boat. When we went in, we found five inches of water standing on the floor. The water finally drained off in a few days, but it left the wood floors warped and buckled.

The children's school reopened before we were able to return home, so they went to school without uniforms. We returned to live at Pontchartrain Park after an eight-day sojourn at my parents' house. The musty odor lingered in our home for weeks, despite scrubbing, despite disinfectants and deodorants, despite repeated airing. Though the memory of Betsy has faded over the years, it was a massive storm that took more than a hundred lives and devastated the Ninth Ward. When it passed, we thought we would never see the likes of it again. About that, we were wrong.

⚜

Jean was with us at our parents' home waiting out the hurricane. She had been living in Memphis, where she was associate librarian at LeMoyne College. I think she enjoyed being there. Jean had an effervescent personality. She liked parties and enjoyed a busy social life in Memphis. It must have been bittersweet, in some ways, to return to New Orleans. Here, though, she had family support, and our father could monitor her condition. All through her life, Jean had difficulty with her leg. Surgery had failed to solve the problem. But early on, we realized it would not stop her. Her disability resulted not in shyness or introversion, but a calculated battle to make the least of her problem. I remember shopping with her as a teenager. She had to wear special shoes that were rather unattractive and dowdy for a young girl. She would bring me with her on these excursions and interrogate me about how each pair of shoes looked: "Are these all right? How about these?" I would try to help her selection as best I could: "Maybe that pair would do. Let's look for another color."

During her early twenties, though, Jean began to be afflicted with benign tumors in various places—on her lung, her kidney, her adrenal gland. All these required surgery. We didn't know yet that she suffered from a fairly rare genetic disease, neurofibromatosis, or Recklinghausen's disease as yet unidentified. That would explain the tumors that plagued her and, possibly, the abnormality of her leg.

Over the years, our father had sought consultations with physicians all over the country about Jean's illnesses. As a physician, he found her condition so painful. I could see it in his face each time she was in crisis. In private, we always feared that one of the tumors would be malignant or in an inoperable place.

In February 1967, Jean woke up with a swollen face. Every diagnostic test available at that time was employed, but diagnostics were limited then, and the doctors couldn't find the cause. Finally, they did exploratory surgery and discovered a malignancy.

Initially, my father did not want to tell Jean about it. At that time, cancer was rarely curable. Then he realized that she was so smart and so well read that she would know immediately when she had to go for radiation. Her surgeon ended up telling her the gravity of her illness; she accepted it stoically.

I know now that my father was trapped in denial. During this, Jean's last illness, he was just devastated. He said to me, holding back tears, "I should be able to heal her, and I can't."

Every other night, after I settled my children into their evening routines, I would visit her. On alternate nights, we collaborated on the

Jean and Sybil in 1949
AUTHOR'S COLLECTION

phone about the day's crossword puzzle in the newspaper; she had always completed it, and I would need her to give me the words I missed.

Daddy told me to be open if she seemed to want to talk, but Jean never talked about her illness, whatever she was feeling. One evening, though, she said to me, "It's a strange feeling. Each time I go for the radiation treatments, I know I might not see someone I saw the last time there."

As she continued her treatments, she developed a kind of funny, obsessive interest in claiming a cashmere sweater offered by the S&H catalog. She said to me, "Sybil, I want this sweater. You have to give me all your S&H stamps so I can add them to mine, and then I can get it."

Maybe she thought she would live longer, or maybe hope was a necessity for her to bear the prognosis. I gave her every Green Stamp I could find.

By June, we knew her time was coming to an end. She wanted to die at home, and she did, on July 14, 1967. She was young, just thirty-five years old.

In retrospect, I think it may have been providential that neither she nor the family knew what her prognosis was when she was growing up. Otherwise, she might not have had the courage to live the full life she did. She was a beautiful person; she enriched my life in so many ways. I still miss her all the time, still think to ask her questions about memories only she and I shared.

If not me, who? If not now, when?

Rabbi Hillel

CHAPTER 14

The Gamble

During his three years as assistant United States attorney, Dutch watched the demographics of New Orleans change. By 1967, it became apparent to him—although to practically no one else—that there was potential for a black candidate to win a seat in the Louisiana House of Representatives. His eyes were on the Second Ward in Orleans Parish (New Orleans), where registered Negro voters now held a slight majority. Even his sympathetic friends, however, expressed doubt that he could win a legislative seat in a district that was the traditional domain of two powerful political families, the Comiskeys and the Burkes. Dutch, though, believed he could convince voters that, given his particular background, he had the commitment and experience to represent them.

He set up his campaign in storefront headquarters on Dryades Street (now Oretha Castle Haley Avenue), a street that had been picketed during the early sixties. From his NAACP years, he knew the community's leadership, including its labor and school leaders and ministers. But he also knew ordinary people and was comfortable talking to just about anyone. He visited churches, stores, even bars in the area. His campaign set up coffee klatches in houses and apartments. Eventually, rallies were held in our small headquarters and in church halls.

I set up a phone bank in the campaign headquarters. My lifelong friend Lydia Sindos Adams recruited some of our friends and other residents of the district. I had known Lydia since we shared exclusive membership in the Merrymakers Club, our homegrown version of a juvenile bridge club. We had plenty of experience getting connected; we contacted virtually every working telephone number in the ward at least one time. Although we had no particular experience in political campaigns, our instincts turned out to be on target. Still, given that Dutch was attempting to take over a traditionally white-held position, he faced considerable opposition. Enthusiasm for his candidacy grew each day, though, because he brought a sense of hope to the community. He talked about specific problems. He had been poor growing up and could speak to the ranks of the impoverished and marginalized.

During the campaign, the all-white International Longshoremen's Association (ILA) held its traditional cocktail party at the ILA Hall on Jackson Avenue in the ward. All of the political heavies were there, including the incumbent state representative, Stephen K. Daley, who introduced himself to me. We exchanged small talk for a minute, and then he smiled oddly at me.

"You know, Mrs. Morial, after I win reelection, I'm going to send you and Dutch on a nice trip to the Bahamas."

I returned his smile. "Your offer is very generous, Mr. Daley, but we will pay for our own victory vacation."

Daley walked away looking stunned and considerably less confident.

⚜

By election eve, emotions in the district reached a crescendo. If Dutch won, he would be the first Negro to be elected to the Louisiana

legislature since Reconstruction, the only black among the 105 representatives. Such a victory would mark a new era in politics in New Orleans and Louisiana.

A frenzied Election Day began with our workers phoning and dis-
tributing neighborhood assignments and election materials. A midday
rally at headquarters spilled onto the street. When the polls closed at
eight that night, campaign workers began to gather. We had no time to go
home to freshen up. Everyone raced to headquarters to see the precinct-
by-precinct results on our two small-screen televisions. We stood silent,
barely breathing, then heard that the final results from all precincts in the
Second Ward were Ernest Morial, 2601; Stephen Daley, 1952; Lawrence
Wheeler, 107. Dutch had won a seat in the Louisiana legislature.

Jubilation broke out—shouting, crying, embracing, dancing. Dutch
hugged me and whispered, "We did it!" He kissed me on the cheek and
went out front to claim victory. More than five minutes passed before the
jubilation quelled enough that he could speak and thank people for their
support. He pledged he would keep his campaign promise to represent
the citizens and their needs in Baton Rouge. The celebration went on for
another hour, supporters and friends all trying to get close to him—to
embrace him and pat him on the back, to say a word of congratulations.
It was their victory, too. And they were fueled by it.

Still, trouble lay ahead. Six days after Dutch won the election, his
victory was challenged in court on the grounds that he did not live in the
district, even though we had an apartment there. Court challenges were
nothing new to us, or to anyone who worked for those who sought equal
representation and participation. And of course, Dutch, in his thorough
planning, always anticipated any obstacles that might snatch success and
victory. He had trained with the best—A. P. Tureaud, Thurgood Marshall, Constance Baker Motley. He was always prepared for the worst and
was a veteran in the courtroom. Thanks to the solidarity of the black attorneys in the city, a decision was rendered in Dutch's favor. We breathed

a huge sigh of relief. His election was validated. Louisiana had turned a page. Or so we believed.

Shortly after the election, I was getting ready to go to bed when the phone rang. I picked it up and heard Dutch's voice.

"What time is it? Where are you?" I asked.

"I'm in Central Lockup," he said flatly. "I've been arrested."

But you just got elected to the legislature, I thought. *You just went to a dinner with the governor.*

"What did you do?"

I listened as patiently as I could to his explanation. That evening, Dutch and his friend Henry Dejoie had attended a fundraiser for Governor John McKeithen at a downtown hotel. After the event, he and Henry went to our apartment in the Second Ward. As they were leaving, they stopped to talk to a neighbor in front of the apartment. A police car drove up, and two policemen stepped out. They told Dutch and Henry that they had to move on. When Dutch asked why, the policemen told them that they were loitering.

"*Loitering?* You were in front of your own house!" I was shouting.

"That's what I said. I told them, 'This is my residence, and I am standing in front of it. I am not loitering.' "

"Then what happened?"

"The two policemen pushed us against the car. They frisked us."

"My God." I couldn't believe what he was saying. He was an elected official!

"I kept saying that we weren't breaking any law and they were making a big mistake."

"Did you tell them you are a legislator?"

"Yes. I tried to show them my legislature card. They wouldn't take it. They just threw us into the back of the police car."

"Oh, Dutch." I was starting to feel sorry for him. "Where are you now?"

"On a pay phone. They charged us with loitering and resisting arrest. They're keeping us in a holding room. They allowed me one call. This is it, Sybil."

When I got off the phone with Dutch, I immediately contacted our district councilman, who called Central Lockup and had Dutch and Henry released.

It wasn't until later the next day that the media reported the incident. It caused a big flap in the police department because an elected official had been arrested on frivolous charges. When Dutch was questioned after the arrest, he stated that this kind of action occurred far too often in the black community. Usually, it was visited on innocent people who had no recourse, because they did not have the contacts or resources to get out of jail on bail or to retain an attorney to challenge the charges. He said that, in many cases, the persons arrested were detained on frivolous charges over the weekend and into the week and as a result lost their jobs because they were absent. Afterward, they feared they would have a police record that would damage their potential for finding new jobs.

Oddly, getting arrested provided Dutch a real opportunity to represent his constituency. He later stated publicly that his arrest exposed an unacceptable practice—today referred to as "racial profiling"—and that he did not regret that it happened. Several days later, police superintendent Joseph Giarrusso offered a public apology.

Shortly after his legislative victory in 1967, Dutch was invited to speak to the New Orleans Press Club. It was the first time a black person had been asked to participate either as speaker or journalist. I attended with him. Dutch took many questions about how he had achieved success in the legislative race and what his priority as a legislator would be. He answered each question with aplomb.

One journalist pointedly asked him, "Mr. Morial, when do you think there will be a black mayor of New Orleans?"

"Maybe in ten years," Dutch said.

It was a prophecy.

Dutch encountered many incidents of racism in the legislature, although they were not overt enough to attract the attention of the media. Some legislators refused to speak to Dutch or shake his hand. Some, when realizing they were walking toward him, made a right-angle turn to avoid an encounter. For the most part, the Orleans Parish delegation, both individually and as a group, was cordial. One legislator, Eddie Booker, Dutch's loyal colleague, supporter, and friend, was his roommate in Baton Rouge during the legislative session.

When the 1968 legislative session convened at the State Capitol, Dutch and several of the Orleans Parish delegation were standing around chatting. A House member from Jefferson Parish walked up to the group, looked around, and asked, "Where's the nigger? If you guys had stuck together, we wouldn't have that nigger in here with us." He hadn't recognized Dutch standing among them.

The media was ever-present during Dutch's first session, observing his every move and action. The first order of business was to elect the speaker of the House, and the leading candidate was reputed to have racist interests. Dutch did not abstain but voted for him; he would pick his battles, and this one was not significant enough to take on.

Another cause was more important to him. In Louisiana, donated blood was marked "White" or "Negro." In 1970, Dutch coauthored a bill to discontinue such labeling. This caused a maelstrom in the House, and a number of legislators rushed up to the rostrum to oppose the bill.

One legislator from Bogalusa ranted, "My grandfather fought in the Civil War . . . for what we thought was our freedom of choice. I don't want no nigger blood in my veins and I refuse to have it. I'd see my family die and go to eternity before I'd have . . . a drop of nigger blood in their veins."

A New Orleans House member, Representative Salvatore Anzelmo, followed the Bogalusa legislator to the podium. "I am sorry you had to

Dutch shows Marc and Jacques how to cast a vote in the Louisiana legislature, 1968.
AUTHOR'S COLLECTION

hear that, Dutch," he said. "There are many of us that are embarrassed by his outburst."

The debate made national news. Shortly afterward, the offending legislator became very ill and sent word that he wanted Dutch to see him in Bogalusa, a hotbed of white resistance and racial violence, but he died before Dutch could visit him.

The blood-labeling bill needed 53 votes to pass. Forty-two of the 105 House members voted in favor of the resolution. Thirty voted against, while 33 were absent and did not vote. The bill failed to pass.

Five years later, though, on May 24, 1975, by Act 638 of the Louisiana legislature, a policy was enacted to accord equal protection under state laws to all citizens without regard to race, creed, color, or national origin and to repeal the laws inconsistent with this policy. The blood-labeling law and all other discriminatory laws were repealed with this act.

Dutch also urged the passage of the Twenty-sixth Amendment to the United States Constitution, which gave eighteen-year-olds the right to vote. The Vietnam War was raging by then, and he believed that if young people were old enough to fight and put their lives on the line, they deserved to vote. He also cosponsored a bill to repeal the death penalty, which failed by a vote of sixty-eight to twenty-six. To this day, the death penalty is still the law of the land in Louisiana.

Marc was ten years old when Dutch was elected to the legislature. As soon as school was out, he went to Baton Rouge with his father with as much enthusiasm as his friends displayed in going off to summer camp. When Marc was twelve, State Senator William Guste, also from New Orleans, appointed him as page, the first time a black youth held that position. That year, Marc spent most of his time on the Senate side, while his father was on the House side.

On the last night of the legislative session, the phone rang a little after midnight. I was startled, fearing that something was wrong, but Marc was shouting excitedly, "Guess what? Senator Jumonville just threw a plate at the clock on the Senate wall to stop it so the filibuster could continue. There is pandemonium here."

I asked where his father was. When he said Dutch was in the House, I told him to go over to meet him there.

"Mom, this is history," he responded. "You can't ask me to miss this."

I didn't realize it at the time, but this was a prelude to a career.

Dutch served in Baton Rouge for three years, and in that time he made his mark. Among other things, he suggested to Governor John McKeithen that he appoint a black judge, and McKeithen did. Israel Augustine was named to the criminal-court bench in New Orleans, the first black person to serve as a judge in Louisiana.

⚜

Early during Dutch's term in the legislature, I was working in the den when I was distracted by the repeated beeping of the television. The net-

The day before his assassination, Martin Luther King Jr. arrives at the airport in Memphis with Andrew Young and Ralph Abernathy.
UNIVERSITY OF MEMPHIS LIBRARIES/PRESERVATION & SPECIAL COLLECTIONS/
MEMPHIS PRESS-SCIMITAR COLLECTION

work was interrupting its programming for a special news report: "Martin Luther King has been shot to death in Memphis."

I could hardly grasp the words: *Martin Luther King has been shot to death in Memphis.*

Dutch was in the study. I called to him, and he came and stood by me.

"Martin has been killed." I could hardly say the words; I could hardly believe it. Not Martin. Dutch and I watched the gruesome footage in silence.

In 1968, there were so many voices of anger and violence, but Martin had not been one of them. And yet there he lay bleeding to death on that hotel balcony. He knew it was his time. He had said it: "Well, I don't know what will happen now; we've got some difficult days ahead. But it really doesn't matter with me now, because I've been to the mountaintop. And I don't mind. Like anybody, I would like to live a long life—longevity has its place. But I'm not concerned about that now. I just want to do God's will. And He's allowed me to go up to the mountain. And I've looked over, and I've seen the Promised Land. I may not get there with you. But I want you to know tonight, that we, as a people, will get to the Promised Land."

He knew it, but we didn't. And we didn't understand his death. I was inconsolable.

I remembered one special time Martin and I had talked. I knew he was coming to New Orleans and had invited him to dinner. He called when he arrived in the city and said that he wanted to come, but he was meeting with some ministers here. It was in New Orleans on that day—January 10, 1957—that the Southern Christian Leadership Conference was born.

I said to Dutch, "Now that Martin is gone, what will become of the movement?"

"It will go on. It must."

And it did. But in the aftermath of Martin's assassination, riots broke out in cities across America. There was too much anger—anger born out of years of rejection and discrimination, anger for our hopes lost in Martin's death. It had to be released. I knew it did. *But like this?*

> *The real safeguard of democracy therefore is education.*
>
> President Franklin Roosevelt,
> September 1936

> *Freedom is not enough.*
>
> President Lyndon Johnson,
> June 1965

CHAPTER 15

The Invitation

One evening after Dutch had been elected to the legislature but not yet sworn in, I was bustling around the kitchen trying to prepare dinner when the phone rang. Cheri was entertaining herself in her playpen. Jacques was playing ball across the street in the park, and Julie and Marc had not yet arrived home from school. I figured it was Dutch wanting to know what was on the menu.

I barely got the receiver to my ear when he blurted, "Sybil, we're invited to dinner at the White House."

"Tonight? I've already started dinner. What white house?"

"The one where the president of the United States lives—you remember, big Texan. Elected three years ago."

"I have to sit down for this." I turned off the range, wiped my hands, and found a place to steady myself at the breakfast table. "Start from the beginning. How were we invited? Are you sure about this, Dutch?"

"Yes, I'm sure."

"Well, how do you know?"

"The usual way, Sybil. We got an invitation."

"Are you sure?"

"I have the envelope in my hand."

"What does it say? Details. I need details."

"I'll show you when I get home."

I'm a fairly methodical cook, but I could not concentrate on getting dinner ready that night. I stood fumbling with the vegetables while all sorts of grand images flooded my mind.

Dutch arrived not long after I hung up the phone. In his hand was a formal engraved envelope, our names sketched elegantly with a calligraphy pen. The dinner was just ten days away. Even though a telephone number was listed, I knew a written invitation required a written response. I scrambled through the pages of *Emily Post Etiquette* and learned that the reply should be in the same format as the invitation. On fine paper stock, I wrote out, "Mr. and Mrs. Ernest N. Morial accept with pleasure the kind Invitation of President and Mrs. Lyndon Baines Johnson to Dinner in honor of Prime Minister and Mrs. Harold Wilson, United Kingdom, on Thursday, the 18th day of January at seven in the evening."

The mail would get to the White House just a couple of days before the event, but in time. I could scarcely believe it. To get some advice, I called around to my well-heeled acquaintances to see if any had ever been to a White House state dinner. Regrettably, no one had. I was on my own.

"Should I wear black tie or white tie and tails?" Dutch asked. The invitation didn't specify dress.

"When you call to RSVP, ask what the attire is. Then we won't have to wonder if we're dressed right," I told him.

⚜

I had read that United States presidents brought their own style to social events. Some were formal, others less so. As a man of that time, Dutch had few choices; my options were more open. I never like to shop at the last minute, so I first took stock of what I had. New Orleans is a Mardi Gras ball town, so I kept several formal dresses. Two white gowns were possibilities. One was a billowy chiffon with a wide, heavily beaded waistband; the other was a white peau de soie I had bought recently. The latter had velvet details in a princess style with a beaded short wrap. It seemed more appropriate. I knew I couldn't find something I liked as much in a short shopping trip. Dutch agreed that it was perfect. (My husband was a natty dresser and often bought wonderful clothes for our daughters and me.) My sister-in-law, Carmen, loaned me her white peau de soie formal coat. Together, the dress and coat made a graceful ensemble.

We arrived in Washington on a Wednesday afternoon and were confronted by a brisk winter wind. Louisiana is usually mild in January, but Washington was bitter. We were happy to settle into our warm hotel room.

Dutch began to unpack. "We should call Hale Boggs before the workday ends." He handed me the number.

Hale was our congressman and House majority whip. I dialed the number and was transferred to his line right away.

"What brings you and Dutch to Washington?" he asked. "How long will you be here?"

I explained we were there to attend a state dinner at the White House.

"Well, you and Dutch are stepping in some high cotton," he responded. "Not many are so privileged and honored—and with the prime minister of the U.K. to boot! That's some mighty high cotton!"

It was wonderful to hear Hale's good wishes. I knew his wonderful wife, Lindy, would also be cheering for us. She, too, had an acute sense of politics and would take over Hale's position some years later. I turned the phone over to Dutch, and he and Hale chatted for a while about Louisiana and New Orleans politics. Then we began to get dressed; our excitement was building by the moment.

We arrived by hired car at the East Gate of the White House, where our identification was checked. The driver was permitted to enter the White House grounds and drop us off at the entrance. Pre-dinner festivities were held in the East Room. We entered on the ground floor and were greeted by a host and hostess, who examined our identification again and gave us a small card in an envelope, which revealed our table assignments. Dutch and I surrendered our wraps and moved toward the elegant sweeping staircase. He took my arm, and we ascended to the next level. As we reached the landing, we were asked to identify ourselves once more. We did. Next, we were escorted into the East Room. As we entered, our names were announced on loudspeaker. "The Honorable and Mrs. Ernest Morial" rang out loud and clear. We were led to the receiving line headed by the president. Lyndon Johnson reached out to shake Dutch's hand and said in his characteristic Texas manner, "Hi, neighbor! Welcome to the White House."

Dutch responded, "It's an honor, Mr. President."

Then Johnson extended his hand to me and said, "Mrs. Morial, I welcome you also."

Looking up at Lyndon Johnson, I could not help remembering him as he was a decade before, cajoling votes on the floor of the Senate. So much had happened in his, and our, world since then. The presidency had aged him, but he was still the outsized, vibrant Texan with a voice one could not ignore.

Lady Bird Johnson leaned forward, extended both hands, and warmly welcomed the two of us. In her soft Southern inflection, she said, "We are glad to have you. Have a good time!"

We looked around and listened as the names of the arriving guests were announced. Vice President Hubert Humphrey, cabinet members, ambassadors, senators, congressmen, captains of industry, labor union

presidents, college presidents, writers, and even a few movie stars milled about the room, chatting with one another. Hale Boggs was right; it was definitely some high cotton. Strangely, I did not see Prime Minister Harold Wilson or his wife during the reception. We would see them at dinner.

The East Room was resplendent; the tall windows were bedecked with brocade draperies, and beautiful flowers adorned the room. I had admired Lady Bird's interest and accomplishment in beautifying the roadways of the West. I could sense her hand in this interior design.

Waiters in black jackets, white shirts, and white gloves asked for our drink preferences, then delivered the beverages accordingly. We introduced ourselves to several guests, including Charles Schultz, the creator of the *Peanuts* cartoon strip. Other guests introduced themselves to us. Everyone seemed pleased to be there. Of the 140 guests, three other couples were black: Margaret and Whitney Young, Vivien and Carl Rowan, and Benetta and Walter Washington. The United States Marine Band, in formal uniform, played show tunes in the background. It was a dignified but buoyant gathering.

I excused myself to go to the restroom before dinner. When I returned, Dutch looked at me inquisitively. "You were gone so long that I thought you must have been checking out the plumbing. I was getting a little worried."

"I did check it out, and all is well."

Like most visitors, I had an insatiable curiosity about the inner workings of the White House and had spent some time looking around, taking in the marble floor and counters, the framed mirrors, and the linen towels with their White House monograms.

After about twenty minutes, the band struck a chord and an announcement was made: "Dinner is served."

We were led into the State Dining Room, where round tables of eight were set with exquisite White House china (simple and elegant cream with a gold band), silver, beautiful leaded glass stemware, and more gorgeous floral arrangements. The engraved dinner menus sat in silver holders next to the place cards, also in silver holders. Husbands and wives were assigned to different tables, a custom at all White House dinners.

The meal comprised six courses: appetizer, soup, sorbet, entrée, salad, dessert, and coffee. The details of each course are vague in my memory, but I do remember that the salad was served after the entrée in continental style, not before, as was our custom. The waiters kept our wineglasses replenished with fine red and white wines. Conversation among the diverse diners at our table was spirited, meandering through a variety of topics. However, there was only guarded mention of Vietnam, which cast a huge shadow over the White House at that time.

The president of the Communications Workers of America, Joseph Beirne, sat next to me; he and I chatted about New Orleans and our children. On my other side was Walter Washington, the appointed mayor of Washington, D.C., whose wife, Benetta, I had met on Dr. and Mrs.

Thomas's yacht when Dutch and I lived in Maryland. Benetta was an activist in the community, both in Alexandria, Virginia, and Washington. We had a connection. Our conversation on the yacht in 1955 had led to her recommending me for a teaching position at the Burgundy Farms Country Day School in Northern Virginia, which at that time had no Negro teachers. She knew about the Newton Public Schools, where I had just taught. After several interviews at Burgundy, I had been offered the job, but I did not want to commute from Baltimore to Alexandria, an hour-and-fifteen-minute drive each way. Some members of the Burgundy Farms School Board were influential; through their political connections, they tried to have Dutch reassigned to Washington, a much shorter commute. He was in army intelligence, however, and there was no counterpart in Washington. The army declined to reassign him, and I did not take the job. Still, I was flattered to have been offered a position at such a progressive and well-regarded school.

I cast a glance around the dining room to spy what my husband was up to. Dutch was at another table with Secretary of Defense Robert McNamara and other notables. Vice President Hubert Humphrey, at an adjacent table, leaned over to Dutch to exchange greetings. President Johnson and Lady Bird and Mr. and Mrs. Harold Wilson sat at the head table. It was round, just like ours, and placed in front of the unlit fireplace, where all diners could see the heads of state.

At the conclusion of the meal, toasts were offered. The president rose with Lady Bird at his side and asked everyone else to stand as he offered a toast to the queen of England. Prime Minister Wilson and Mrs. Wilson stood.

"To the queen of England! Hear, hear!"

Everyone repeated the toast with gusto, followed by the clink of glasses.

"To Great Britain! Hear, Hear!"

Again, all joined in avidly, with more clinking after the toast.

"To Prime Minister Wilson! Hear, hear!"

The prime minister, his wife standing next to him, offered a toast, again echoed with enthusiasm: "To the United States of America! Hear, hear!"

"To President Lyndon Johnson! Hear, hear!"

A robust response to the final toast and a last clinking of glasses ended the dinner.

The president then led everyone back to the East Room for dancing. We all walked leisurely and chatted along the way. The Marine Band was playing dance music, but no one dared dance before the president stepped onto the floor.

But he didn't dance. He left. Protocol dictates that when the president leaves, the party is over. So we all descended that grand staircase, those of us who were there for the first time still marveling at an extraordinary experience. The glow of touching a world of executive privilege for the first time warmed us as we faced the cold January night.

The Rowans invited us for a nightcap at their home. The Youngs joined us. Carl Rowan was a noted journalist and director of the United States Information Agency. Whitney Young was executive director of the National Urban League and was in the process of transforming the league into a powerful proactive organization. Our conversations were about the movement, especially the rise in black voters and black elected officials since the Voting Rights Act was passed. Of course, Dutch's election was representative of that trend.

Dutch and I went back to our hotel feeling the warm glow of an extraordinary evening and slept comfortably in our bed.

That was the first time we were guests at the White House; happily, it would not be the last.

If Liberia has failed, then it is no evidence of the failure of the Negro in government. It is merely the evidence of the failure of slavery.

Carter G. Woodson

CHAPTER 16

Into Africa

For many of us involved in the United States Civil Rights Movement, the decades between 1950 and 1970 were principally about the struggle for equal rights in our own country. While we embraced African clothing, music, and styles, few of us grasped the wide range of nations and cultures that existed, and were dynamically evolving, on the African continent. Nor were many of us aware of the conflicts, sometimes violent, that were part of the quest for political identity and self-determination in the face of continuing colonialism and international economic tyranny. It was at heart a massive struggle for dignity and political power, and it was unnervingly complex.

Even within Africa itself, few books were written about these ongoing crises. Occasionally, however, especially when violence was involved, stories of the struggles appeared in the media. When Congo gained independence from Belgium—after a hundred years of brutal colonial oppression—the accompanying violence against Belgian settlers was a cover story, making it into the pages of *Life* magazine. Congo was not the first African nation to assert its identity, and it would not be the last. All over the continent, African nations were declaring their independence. Ongoing struggles for liberation were rarely bloodless and sometimes murderous.

As African nations fought for political control, the economics, the borders, and even the names of nations changed. American ignorance of Africa, among both whites and Negroes, continued to be profound. We didn't know about Africa, but Africa knew about us. The connection was as wide and deep as the Middle Passage.

Our education about the continent—there was little early education about distinct African nations, except for Egypt—was veiled in a fog of stereotypes. I still remember cringing in my high school world geography class when Bertha Magrauer, an otherwise superb teacher, began her lecture about Africa by saying, "The next continent we will learn about is the Dark Continent, the place of your ancestors." As was her style, she uttered this line with great drama. Our class, comprised of young Negroes, adopted a look of profound objection. Quiet mumblings ensued. "Dark Continent" conjured up secret, sinister images. We became uncomfortable. We had learned about slavery and accepted our African origins, but we did not think of ourselves as Africans. The name at that point conjured images from Tarzan movies—minimally dressed natives with spears, struggling to speak the barest phrases of pigeon English. We knew little or nothing about early civilizations in North Africa and sub-Saharan Africa and the contributions they made to the world. We knew nothing about European colonization and the exploitation of labor and natural resources in those countries. That history was not in school textbooks.

I still shudder to consider how this brainwashing fed us inaccurate information about our heritage and history, giving us a negative image of our origins and influencing white Americans' attitudes toward people of

African descent, thus reinforcing their bias and prejudice.

We Negro students were embarrassed to claim African heritage. It would be decades before Eastern civilization courses would be taught alongside Western civilization. When Ghana, formerly the Gold Coast, adjacent to the Ivory Coast, became independent in 1957—the first former European colony in Africa to do so—our eyes began to open. Before that, we truly were "in the dark."

For that matter, we thought of ourselves as Americans. We were civilized, well dressed, clean, and combed; we were literate, well educated. While the "Dark Continent" reference conjured up threatening images, we at Xavier Preparatory saw ourselves as the noonday sun.

⚜

Arriving at Boston University in 1950, I had been lucky enough to share my dorm room with Izetta Roberts from Liberia, West Africa, a country founded by ex-slaves transferred from America beginning in 1820. Izetta's family had been involved in Liberian politics—her late father was a senator in the Liberian Parliament—and Izetta was generous in teaching me not only about her own country but also about other nations in Africa.

Through her, I came to understand the longstanding tensions of colonialism that would continue to the end of the century and beyond. More importantly, Izetta opened Africa's bright doors for me. She introduced me to other African students from various nations. Through them, I began to learn about individual national cultures and African diversity from country to country.

In 1972, two decades after I graduated from Boston University, Dutch and I traveled to Liberia to attend the inauguration of its newly elected president, William R. Tolbert. Dutch was representing the Alpha Phi Alpha fraternity as its general (international) president. There was an organization chapter in Monrovia, Liberia's capital.

Roberts Airport in Monrovia, where we landed, was comparatively small. Deplaning, we entered a one-story lobby/waiting room filled with people. Most of the travelers were visitors from other countries intent on attending the inauguration. A member of Dutch's fraternity greeted us and helped us retrieve our luggage and move through customs. Riding in a comfortable sedan through Monrovia (named for President James Monroe), I was shocked to see people living along the road in dilapidated lean-tos. The structures consisted of tin, cardboard, and pieces of wood. People moved about, buying and selling wares.

But there was another Monrovia. When we got into the heart of the city, its scenery improved. The public places and streets were swept and clean, decorated for the festivities of inauguration. Everywhere we turned, dramatic frangipani trees laden with orange, magenta, and white blossoms abounded; bougainvillea vines in stunning colors hung everywhere along the roads. Our windows were open, and the air was intoxicating with the floral fragrance.

Soon after we settled at the home of one of Dutch's fraternity brothers, Izetta called to welcome us and to arrange a time to pick us up and bring us to her home. I was excited to see her in her own country. On the ride to her house, we caught up on our lives, our children. After BU, she had gone to graduate school and studied library science. She had married another American-educated Liberian, Nehemiah Cooper. Her husband was a prominent physician who ran a large medical clinic in Monrovia. He counted as one of his patients the new president.

As we approached Izetta's home, my breath came up short. Her house sat on a hill surrounded by lush trees and shrubs overlooking Guinea Bay. The design was a bit strange to me—thick louvers at the windows but no glass. Izetta told us that tropical weather made glass unnecessary; the angled louvers kept the rain from coming inside.

I noted quite a few servants and wondered what they all did. Izetta told me that each had a specific assignment: laundress, cook, gardener, chauffeur, maid, and nanny. These jobs, she said, enabled them to take care of their families. Jobs were still not plentiful for indigenous Liberians, many of whom lacked higher education and technical training. Using her graduate degree, Izetta was now working toward organizing her country's library system.

In many ways that I did not understand at first, Liberia was still a divided society. In the early nineteenth century, when former slaves from the United States had come to live on the west coast of Africa, the land was already inhabited by groups of indigenous Africans of the Niger-Congo family. Although Liberia declared its independence in 1847, a separation between indigenous people and American Liberians continued. Only in the second half of the twentieth century did Liberian society begin to attain some homogeneity. In 1958, racial discrimination was outlawed, but class and social divisions still existed.

President Tolbert was from Americo-Liberian stock, and his inauguration attracted many influential blacks from the United States. Political figures, journalists, photographers, and educators were all in attendance. Afterward, along with Liberian and other dignitaries, Dutch and I were given a tour of the university and a Firestone rubber plantation, a major employer in Monrovia. Tolbert's inauguration was quite grand, and Dutch and I enjoyed the evening ball.

A few days later, we left Liberia and crossed the border into the Ivory Coast (Côte d'Ivoire), a former French colony that had gained its independence in 1959.

From there, we proceeded to Ghana, where we met up again with members of the Liberian inauguration group. An influential Ghanian with whom we spoke predicted a political coup in the country within the next few days. He advised that we leave as soon as possible. We were startled by this report but were already scheduled to leave the next day for Nigeria. Just as predicted, a coup d'état by the military in Ghana occurred several days later.

Dutch and I returned to Liberia in 1980 on a New Orleans trade

mission. Again, though, violence gripped West Africa. Three weeks after we left Liberia, a bloody coup led by an indigenous military leader
left the country in political unrest for years. President Tolbert was as-
sassinated shortly after we returned to the United States. Because of her
family's position in Monrovia, Izetta was caught up in the turmoil that
followed the assassination. The role of her husband, Nehemiah, as Tolbert's personal physician placed their family in jeopardy. Izetta's cousin
Cecil Dennis, a member of the Liberian foreign ministry, was executed,
along with a dozen others from Tolbert's administration. I was shocked
when I heard this, as Izetta had introduced Cecil to me when we were all
at the university in Boston.

Although her husband had to stay to manage the clinic, Izetta made
clandestine plans to get out of Liberia. She went to Switzerland, where
her daughter Lisa was attending boarding school. Eventually, the family
came to the United States and stayed here, although Nehemiah made oc-
casional trips to maintain the clinic in Monrovia.

It would take decades, but better times would come for Liberia. After years of violence and corruption—including an ongoing civil war—a
group of Liberian women formed the Women of Liberia Mass Action
for Peace. In a brave move, they forced a meeting with then-president
Charles Taylor and made him commit to peace talks. Over three thousand women added their voices demanding the end of violence. Out of
this movement rose a dynamic leader. In 2006, Ellen Johnson Sirleaf became Liberia's president, the first modern elected female head of state in
Africa. Sirleaf would be awarded the Nobel Prize for her efforts for peace.
One of her first moves as Liberia's president was to restore electricity to
the nation. Lights that had not been seen in the streets for years were
turned on again.

Under Sirleaf's leadership, the Liberian economy grew prodigiously
until the Ebola crisis hit West Africa in 2014. With assistance from the
United States and other countries, Liberia surmounted the outbreak,

though over five thousand Liberians lost their lives. By early 2015, the disease seemed to be under control in Liberia, although Sierra Leone and Guinea were still struggling to contain the deadly virus.

Tomorrow,
I'll be at the table
When company comes.
Nobody'll dare
Say to me,
"Eat in the kitchen,"
Then.

Besides,
They'll see how beautiful I am
And be ashamed—

I, too, am America.

Langston Hughes

CHAPTER 17

Where We Began

In 1980, on our second trip to Africa, we visited the West African nation of Senegal for the first time. As we walked through the streets of the capital, Dakar, I was stunned by the beauty of the people in the city, most of whom were tall and dark skinned. They walked in a stately manner, very erect. The men wore tunics and loose pants gathered at the ankles. The women, in colorful, flowing, long dresses, seemed to float through the streets. A certain elegance pervaded the city, highlighted by the French patois spoken by its residents. (The land had been colonized by the Portuguese in 1444, then the Dutch in 1588 and the French in 1677, and although French was the official language, many local languages survived, as well.)

While we were there, Dutch met with the first president of the independent Senegal, Leopold Senghor, who was nearing the end of his term. He was a world-class poet, a vibrant intellectual, and a great statesman who much impressed my husband. Senghor gave us as a gift a copy of a bronze sculpture by the American sculptor Frederic Remington—a bronco on horseback, a lovely reminder of our visit.

Our son Marc accompanied us. He was a senior at the University of Pennsylvania and should have been in classes but had persuaded his advisor to allow a ten-day leave so he could write a paper on African energy sources. Marc was inventive in finding ways to take his education out of the classroom and indulge his love of history and politics. In Senegal, he met with scientists and other officials to learn about solar energy in that nation.

After we toured Dakar, our next destination was Goree, a small Atlantic island at the westernmost point of Africa. The island had served as an embarking point for slave ships bound to North America. Crossing to the island on the ferry, we watched the gentle whitecaps and inhaled the salt breeze. When we disembarked, we walked about a block along a path lined with scrub plants and a lone tall bougainvillea that climbed the side of a building.

Soon, we came upon a large stone structure. The remains of what appeared to be shackles were embedded in the floor. For nearly three centuries, men, women, and children were brought forcibly to this island and sold to European and American slave traders. The tour guide explained that the slaves were corralled and held until the next slave ship arrived. On the far side of the building was a large opening onto the Atlantic. The slaves were taken along a short gangplank into the hold of the ship. The guide called it "the Door of No Return," as those African people would never see their homeland again. The building was a memorial to all those who had been brutally captured and sold into slavery, then sent with no hope of return into the horrors of the Middle Passage. The trip to the

Americas would take more than a month. Some, perhaps many, would not survive. Those who did would face a life they did not want to live.

Being confined in that space, feeling the metal at my feet, sent a deep chill through my body. I turned to Marc, and we glanced at each other in horror. Dutch and I had previously visited Elmina, a major slaveholding and boarding area in Ghana, but our journey to Goree affected me with a haunting immediacy in a way Elmina had not.

❧

Growing up, I had learned about Negroes and slavery gradually. Our textbooks dealt with slavery from the owners' perspective; the slaves' personal lives were never considered, their names deleted.

My maternal ancestry remained mostly a mystery. My maternal grandmother, Antoinette Jones Arnaud, had three children—my mother, Eudora, and her two brothers, Archie, the oldest child, and Lester, the youngest. Uncle Archie was a school principal who had earned a master's degree in 1934; Uncle Lester was a pharmacist. My mother was a teacher until she married. (After teachers married, they were required to resign.) My maternal grandfather, Duke Wellington Arnaud, died when my mother was just twelve years old. After his death, my grandmother sent my mother and her brothers to Waveland, Mississippi, to live with their grandmother, Mary Jones, whom we called Grandma Jones. I got to know these relations because my family and our cousins visited every summer and brought a picnic lunch to enjoy in her beautiful, shady backyard. We picked blackberries and walked the two blocks to the beach to play and swim in the Gulf of Mexico.

While the history of my mother's family remained sketchy, the ancestry of my father, Clarence Haydel, was much more evident. Most of the Haydels, including my father, grew up in Louisiana farm communities along the River Road in the area known as the German Coast, about forty miles upriver from New Orleans. He came from a large extended family that was a fairly constant presence in our lives. His mother, Nellie Ory Haydel, moved from the farm to New Orleans in about 1940 and lived just a few blocks from our house. She was pretty, a gentle lady who wore a single-strand pearl necklace and matching earrings whenever she came to our house. When we visited her, she was always bustling at the stove. Her kitchen was filled with wonderful aromas as we waited in anticipation for her special treat: hot French bread with butter, sugar, and cinnamon.

My father was the oldest of nine children—six boys and three girls. His father, Clay Haydel, died a few months before my sister Jean, his first grandchild, was born. Because we regularly visited the family farm, I knew how different life was for Negroes outside the city. Rituals of farm life hadn't changed much since Reconstruction. My father's brother Earlric went along with my father to New Orleans to be educated, but he didn't choose city life. He returned home to farm his own land along the River Road, which since plantation times has tracked the Mississippi from New Orleans to Baton Rouge.

My sister and I visited Earlric (we called him "Uncle Wick") for a week every summer. He raised standard southern Louisiana crops— sugarcane and rice and vegetables. On our visits to the farm, Jean and I would walk along the path next to the sugarcane field performing our main chore—picking up milk just gotten from the cow, Clarabelle. On the path, we would get nervous because a young farmhand was always jumping out of the cane rows to scare us. He told us ghost stories and frightened us stiff about what might be lurking in that dense cane field.

The levee holding back the Mississippi was just across the road; when we were little, we often romped over it and rolled down its slope. Jean and I loved to play in the haystack left from the threshed rice, but it left us itchy and with straw in our hair and clothes. We would hurry to take a cool bath to soothe our skin. In the evening, when dinner was done and farm chores were over for the day, all of us would sit on the front porch facing the levee. In the cool breeze of evening, Jean and I, along with Aunt Patsy (Uncle Wick's wife) and our cousins, would pass time sifting baskets of rice, taking out the dark blue indigo seeds that often survived the thresher. (Indigo, once a primary crop, had been abandoned in favor of the more lucrative sugarcane; indigo seeds lingered in the soil for years.)

The Mississippi River provided transport for most crops of cane and rice that the old plantations—now much smaller farms—sent to the port of New Orleans. The boats came by to pick up the crops, including those from my father's family farm. Many times, they came at night. Farmers had to wait with their crops on the pier when the river level was high, or otherwise on the *batture*, the dry land between the levee and the low-water level. Uncle Whitney, another of my father's younger brothers, often talked about having to rush the cart loaded with sugarcane to the mournful warning of the boater's horn. The family's mule, Maud, dragged the wagon; she knew the way even in the dark. Uncle Whitney, who left the farm to attend school in New Orleans after fifth grade (education for rural Negroes stopped there), told us how much he longed to go back to the city during those hours. The tedium of the schoolhouse didn't compare to the blind struggle to guide a wagon of cane across the road and up and down the levee in the dark. Eventually, he gave up the rural life.

Uncle Wick, on the other hand, seemed to love the land—it was his, and it yielded a generous crop of sugarcane and a smaller crop of rice each harvest to provide his living.

Our Haydel family was, and still is, huge, with lots of uncles, aunts, and cousins. On Thanksgiving Day, we went to the home of my paternal grandmother, Nellie Ory Haydel—we called her "Gran"—in New Orleans. By then, the entire family including Gran and my father's brothers and sisters, except for Uncle Wick, had moved from the River Road to New Orleans. As we walked in the door, we were embraced by the aroma of gumbo, the staple appetizer before the main course of turkey and Gran's famed oyster dressing. That recipe is the standard holiday fare

in our family to this day. I would watch Gran put filé, the essential pow-
dered sassafras, into the gumbo pot, testing the consistency with each
spoonful she added.

On All Saints' Day, we would take a drive to my paternal grandfather
Clay's grave in the churchyard of St. John the Baptist in Edgard. The Catholic church where my father and his family were baptized sat not far from
the farm where my father had grown up, downriver from Uncle Wick's
land. The graves were in the churchyard. My parents brought lunch—
usually ham sandwiches and fruit—and sat around the graves visiting
with adult cousins. While they chatted, we children played Simon Says
and circle games on the strips of green lawn that lined the graves.

During family get-togethers, the adults loved to talk. When I got to
be about ten or eleven, I intentionally eavesdropped on adult conversations. If I made any noise or tried to join in, they would become silent
or abruptly change the conversation. I heard enough to know there were
secrets in our family, but not enough to make sense of it, just to know
it had to do with my father's family. What I knew about that part of our
family didn't go back very far. I was aware that my father, Clarence, grew
up in Wallace, the oldest of Clay and Nellie's six boys and three girls. I
knew all of these aunts and uncles, but I was told nothing about our earlier ancestors. Jean was as curious as I was, and we talked about what we
had heard, then forgot the issue until the next eavesdropping session. As
young children, we came to understand that some members of the family had light-colored skin, and we assumed we had a mixed heritage with
some European—probably French—blood, as many New Orleanians
did. As far as the law in Louisiana and much of the South was concerned,
we were Negro. The rule was that even one drop of blood made us so.

⚜

In 1981, the year after we visited Africa for the second time, the
Haydels held a family reunion. Nearly two hundred members of the

family—from as far away as California, Michigan, and New York—gathered in Bay St. Louis, Mississippi. During the three days we spent together, I met cousins I hadn't seen since I was a child and other cousins I didn't know at all. By that time, I was intensely curious about relationships within our family; any connections to the past, including those in Africa, intrigued me. My trips there had prompted more curiosity about details of my African roots.

In conversations, we tried to piece together the relationships between family members and our ancestors. Finally, I was able to determine that we were all descendants of one man, a mulatto (a person of mixed Negro and other ancestry). His name was Victor Haydel. Victor was known in the family as "Pépère," a French term meaning "papa" or "grandfather." I had always thought that our white ancestor must be French because my grandmother spoke French. This French term of endearment seemed to confirm that. But it had never occurred to me that Victor's appellation could have come from the French-derived Senegalese, as would later come to light.

Victor's granddaughter, my cousin Sadie, remembered him fondly and mesmerized us with stories about the plantation and our cousins. Sadie told us that Pépère was born in 1835, before the slaves were freed. She didn't say, but I wondered, *Was he a slave?* I had never heard the word spoken in any of the family stories. And I wondered why Victor was the only ancestor the family talked about. Did they not know about his heritage, or were they just not talking about it?

And there was another mystery: If Victor was a mulatto, who was his father? Who was his mother?

The questions haunted me. I was almost fifty years old then, with five children, yet I knew so little about my lineage before my grandfather Clay. The snippets of stories I had overheard began to come together in my mind. Still, I wanted to know details. My father had told us about his youth growing up on the farm, but he never talked about Pépère's origins. After our reunion, though, I began to ask him questions, and he told me several things. Pépère was the son of a black woman who worked in the Haydel plantation house. But I had never been there. My visits were limited to Uncle Wick's farm and St. John the Baptist Church and its graveyard. I remembered knowing the names of the river plantations we drove by on the way to Uncle Wick's house— Oak Alley, Evergreen, and *Haydel*. Our name, but how were we connected to it?

My father answered some of my questions, but I had so many others. Sadly, he died the following year, and his revelations about Victor and his parentage ended. I began putting together pieces of the puzzle through other sources. During the 1990s, my cousin Belmont Haydel began conducting research on our family's history. Using court and church documents, he compiled a genealogical volume of our family.

In 2009, the Haydel family joined for another reunion, attended by 125 family members. We intended to meet at the Haydel plantation, where we had learned our ancestor was born. But it had deteriorated badly, so we met at Evergreen Plantation, a mile or so downriver. At the reunion, Belmont presented his substantial research. Through his detailed explanations, we learned that Pépère had been born and lived on the Haydel plantation, and that he was the son of a woman named Anna. She was a servant to the mistress of the house, Azelie Haydel, the wife of Marcellin Haydel, the plantation's owner at the time. Victor had been fathered by Azelie's brother, Antoine Haydel.

Although I still had many questions, Belmont had finally opened the book of our Haydel origins and tracked them back, ancestor by ancestor, to a German immigrant, Ambroise Heidel, who had come to Louisiana in 1721. By 1752, Ambroise had bought the original land grant and established a huge indigo plantation.

Belmont had also found the matrilineal origin of the African American Haydels. Anna's origins and story, however, remained hidden, as did Victor's status in the Haydel family. I still wondered, *Was he a slave or not?*

Some of the German (white) descendants of Ambroise joined us at the family reunion. They, along with the African American Haydels, cooperated in Belmont's exploration of the family. They provided information about our German ancestry and referred him to sources in Neunkirchen, Germany, the community from which Ambroise emigrated.

Eventually, I began to learn about the evolution of the plantation itself. After the Civil War, Haydel had been sold and renamed Whitney Plantation and continued as farming property. After 1990, it was about to be purchased by commercial interests that planned to put a rayon plant on the farmland. Environmental groups prevented the sale. The big house, built by slave labor and talent and added to the National Register of Historic Places in 1992, is now considered one of the finest surviving examples of Spanish Creole architecture.

During studies for the rayon plant, inventories of slaves were found that detailed their lives on the Haydel plantation. In 1999, New Orleans lawyer John Cummings and his family purchased the property. They had a vision for it. They set about restoring the main buildings and replacing outbuildings such as slave quarters to capture the experience of the plantation when slaves were its lifeblood. Cummings felt a mission to offer this experience as an informed contrast to tours typically offered on the River Road, in which guides emphasized the lives of the planters and often neglected the roles of African, West Indian, and Native American slaves who made the elegant lifestyles—and the essential agricultural production—possible. Now the Whitney Plantation, a museum devoted to the history of slavery in the United States, presents the system of slavery in southern Louisiana, along with the Senegalese and other West and Central African cultures of the slaves who contributed to the formation of Louisiana Creole culture. It also illustrates contributions of those enslaved on Louisiana's German Coast, who were put to work for the comfort and welfare of their owners. According to its description, it is "a site of memory and consciousness [that] pays homage to all slaves who

Slave cabins on the grounds of the former Haydel plantation, now the Whitney Museum
COURTESY OF THE WHITNEY MUSEUM

worked the plantation and to all of those enslaved in the South." John Cummings has described the museum as "no longer a piece of property, but sacred ground."

To fully tell the story of the historic plantation, Cummings and his wife, Donna, procured the services of a Senegalese history professor, Dr. Ibrahima Seck. Now director of the museum, Seck received his doctorate from the University of Dakar. He had explored the slave trade between Senegal and Louisiana/Mississippi in his dissertation. His book, *Bouki Fait Gombo*, about the German Coast plantations and specifically the former Habitation Haydel (as it was formally known), opened a new door in understanding my ancestry, including the connection between the Haydels and Senegal, something I never knew but had perhaps sensed in my spirit as I stared out at the ocean from Goree Island so long ago.

We do not know when Anna arrived at Habitation Haydel, but it was sometime between the 1820 census (she was not listed) and 1835, when Victor was born. Dr. Seck interviewed a family member who had been told that Anna was purchased by Marcellin Haydel in New Orleans and brought home to his wife, Azelie, who was childless. That source also reported that Anna could remember her own mother falling asleep (most likely dying) and dropping off a ship somewhere; Anna grieved that loss and the loss of her brothers, who had traveled with her to Louisiana. She never saw them again. The person who related this story had received it from his parents, who suspected that Anna had been raped, since a slave girl could not have resisted a white man's advances, and since she showed dislike toward Antoine.

At the time Anna came to Habitation Haydel, it had been a thriving plantation for more than eighty years. Domestic slaves such as Anna worked inside the house, but most slaves worked in the fields. In the 1800s, sugar replaced indigo as the main crop. Field slaves did the intense work of clearing dense ground cover, building the levees, planting seedlings, and harvesting the crop.

Victor's and Anna's positions within the Haydel family were an enigma. On one hand, Victor had been fathered by a Haydel, Antoine. On the other hand, he was the child of a Negro or mulatto house servant. Victor was treated better than a slave; he was baptized and was not put to work in the field, but he was not legally treated as family. He was never taught to read or write. Instead, he and his mother were viewed as property.

When Azelie died in 1860, she was the largest slaveholder in the state, owning nearly a hundred slaves. Victor and Anna were assessed as part of the estate. Victor was valued at eight hundred *piastres*, the equivalent of eight hundred dollars, and Anna, his mother, at a hundred *piastres*. We do not know what happened between 1860 and the Emancipation Proc-

Front of the Haydel plantation house
CURTIS GRAVES, PHOTOGRAPHER

lamation in 1863. Anna, like many of those enslaved, simply appeared and then disappeared. Although it is possible that she did not experience a single day of freedom in America, she is the matriarch of our family.

Victor (Pépère) survived to become a free man at the age of twenty-eight. He married another mulatto, Celeste Becnel. Celeste gave birth to one daughter and eight sons, one of whom was my grandfather Clay Haydel, born in 1870. After he was freed, Victor worked hard for several years until he was able to purchase land and begin to farm it. Several of Victor's sons became landowners under the Haydel Brothers Planting Company.

My grandfather Clay owned farmland and was a partner in a grocery store with his wife Nellie's brother Johnny. Nellie's other brother was the celebrated jazz musician Kid Ory, who sometimes played at family gatherings. They were one generation removed from slavery. The next generation—my father's—grew up on the farm. My father was sent to New Orleans to complete his early education, then went on to Howard University Medical School in Washington, D.C. Negroes were not admitted to medical schools in the South.

Many of his siblings and cousins also went to New Orleans to be educated. The grandsons of the slave Victor overcame the brutal years of discrimination and deprivation. They settled in New Orleans. Some became professionals, others successful entrepreneurs. Subsequent generations of Haydels, including my own, have continued to honor the values and traditions of our ancestors through our professions and contributions to our communities.

Dr. Seck wrote, "The best way to honor the memories of Anna, Victor, and Celeste, is to let the world know the hardship they went through and the injustice of being considered chattel for many years with a price imposed on each of them. In doing so, much respect would also be paid to those who sacrificed their lives in the defense of freedom and civil rights in this country and beyond."

You must be the change you wish to see in the world.

Mahatma Gandhi

CHAPTER 18

Race for Mayor

The Louisiana legislature met for its regular session for two months each year, April to June, Monday through Thursday. Sessions were held in the State Capitol in Baton Rouge, seventy miles from New Orleans. Sometimes, additional special sessions required the same attendance.

Dutch's time away from his legal practice was beginning to take its toll on our family income. By then, we had four children—Monique would soon add to that number—and although I was teaching, Dutch needed a steady income. He learned there was a vacancy—a judgeship—for an unexpired term on the juvenile court in New Orleans. Governor John McKeithen appointed Dutch to the position for the remainder of the term—eighteen months. He would have to run for the position when the unexpired term was up.

Juvenile justice was an area that interested Dutch. He wanted to be an advocate for young people who might be going down the wrong track. When his replacement time was up, he ran for a full term and won.

One day, I met Dutch at court to attend an event and witnessed my husband in action. A court officer brought a teenage boy up to the bench on a charge. There was a scuffle, and a second officer ran up and handcuffed the youth. He was accused of carrying a weapon in his back pocket.

Dutch asked to see the weapon. When an Afro pick was presented, Dutch raised his eyebrows. "That is not a weapon. It's a grooming piece."

A bit of black culture was revealed for the benefit of all present.

After three years on the juvenile court, Dutch ran for another judgeship, on the Louisiana Court of Appeals, and won. His tenure beginning in 1974 was a relatively normal time for our family. He was home at a reasonable hour, sat down to dinner four or five times a week, and generally spent more time with me and our five children. Life moved at a slower pace, and I enjoyed it. Still, knowing Dutch, I sensed it was only an interlude.

Throughout the years of our marriage, I came to discern a certain look. Actually, it was more than a look; it was a mood, a disposition that took over Dutch's body. I knew the subtle signs, and when I saw them, I silently braced myself for a new challenge. I wasn't quite prepared, though, when one day after dinner, he said to me, "I think I could be elected mayor of New Orleans."

I was so startled, I just sputtered, "You're dreaming."

"No, Sybil, I'm serious. I've been thinking about it for a while and studying the demographics of the city. I know I can compete with any white candidate. I am as qualified as any, and better qualified than most."

He must have seen the look of disbelief on my face, so he jumped in: "Before you blow up, I want you to know that I have weighed all of the risks for me and for the family."

My mind was racing. I was thinking, *This is huge*. But I interrupted him, "You would give up a secure and prestigious position on the court of appeals for a gamble like a run for mayor? I thought you were intellectually challenged with the work on the court. I thought you were content there." Actually, I had been thinking for the past few months that the calm life of the court was contrary to his impatient nature. "Have you thought about the financial risks? We have two children at Ivy League universities. Will you have to resign to run? My salary is not nearly enough to sustain us while you campaign. What if you don't win? Where do you go from there?"

"Sybil, hear me out! This is not a decision I made hastily. For months, I have been discretely inquiring what I need to do to keep my position on the court after the campaign if I should lose. I knew I would have to convince you that I can win, but also that I can return to the court if I don't."

He went on: "I would have to challenge the statutes that prohibit judges from running for a political office. The law is vague on whether a sitting judge can engage in politics and run for a public office. I have thought of a strategy. I want to take this on."

His premise was that, in order to be elected, judges did in fact have to run for office. Judicial candidates had to raise money and solicit support; that was, in essence, engaging in politics. Dutch was a strong believer in the American judicial system, and he wanted to test the law.

Cheri and Monique walked in. We ended the conversation there.

During the hours before bedtime, I had a little time to think. I considered what Dutch had said. My initial reaction was, *Can he win at this time in a majority-white city?* I knew he could get some white support. The possibility of his being elected mayor was not entirely outrageous. Several African Americans had been elected mayors of big cities—Carl Stokes in Cleveland, Richard Hatcher in Gary, Indiana, and Maynard Jackson in Atlanta, another Southern city.

I turned over in my mind how, in previous challenges except for a run for city council in 1970 that he admitted was ill timed, Dutch had been successful. He had an uncanny instinct about politics. But I saw the risks for the family. This proposition was huge. I was just about to begin my new career at Xavier University as director of special services. I wondered how this decision would affect my career. There was so much to consider.

That night in bed, we resumed the conversation. He said, "Sybil, do you think I haven't considered the effect on the family if I run for mayor? Yes, there is a risk. I will do all I can to minimize the risk. But I want a chance. I have a vision for this city."

He spoke so passionately that I could not help being captivated by his enthusiasm. By the time the conversation ended, I was convinced he had a chance. I said, "Yes, I'm in. Let's do it," and turned off the light.

So off we went on the most challenging race we had ever undertaken. The primary was scheduled for October 1 and the general election for November 12.

Dutch communicated with the Louisiana Judiciary Commission, which had supervision over the judiciary in the state, to clarify the requirement for a judge to resign from the court twenty-four hours before running for a political office. He was told that the requirement held.

He made a strategic decision to challenge the commission in federal court rather than state court because he thought he would have a better shot at a favorable decision. In February 1977, a team of attorneys led by Trevor Bryant, Sidney Bach, and David Marcello filed a suit brought by a host of plaintiffs (including my cousin Wellington Arnaud) against the Louisiana Judiciary Commission in United States District Court. The case was assigned to Judge Fred Cassibry's section, a serendipitous stroke of luck, since Judge Cassibry had run for a state district judgeship before he was appointed to the federal bench by President Lyndon Johnson. His campaign had involved securing support and raising money, which was the premise of Dutch's suit. Judge Cassibry had also been a member of the New Orleans City Council. He decided in Dutch's favor and enjoined the commission from enforcing the resignation requirement. The Louisiana Judiciary Commission filed an appeal in the United States Fifth Circuit Court of Appeals, where it was argued in June before

THE WEEKLY NEWSPAPER OF ● NEW ORLEANS

courier the

WEEK OF MARCH 24–30, 1977

FIRST BLACK MAYOR ?

Dutch during campaign for mayor, 1977
COURIER WEEKLY NEWSPAPER

a three-judge panel. The court took the appeal under advisement.

In the meantime, Dutch quietly gathered support. When he approached friends and supporters from previous races, not a few asked if he had lost his mind. But others—Don Bernard, Harriett Burnett, Ronald Gardener, Russell Henderson, Mary Ethel Siefkin, Novyse Soniat, and Paul Valteau—immediately pledged support and organized the campaign structure. Philip Baptiste and Leah and Dooky Chase were the first contributors to the campaign fund. In a short time, inspired by Dutch's enthusiasm, many doubters got on board.

In 1977, some 43 percent of New Orleans registered voters were African American and 57 percent white. In order to be victorious, Dutch had to win significant votes in the African American community and some votes in the white community as well.

By August, there was still no decision from the three-judge appellate panel. Dutch took a leave of absence without pay to announce his candidacy and began campaigning vigorously. He established his campaign headquarters in the grand historic Claver Building, across the street from the Lafitte public-housing development. It had been built in 1861 as a hospital for French-speaking New Orleanians. In 1949, it was purchased by the Knights of Peter Claver, a black Catholic organization. Since then, it had been divided into offices, some of which had served to launch important civil rights battles. Dutch's and A. P. Tureaud's law offices were there, as well as the offices of the Urban League and the NAACP.

Marc was then a sophomore at the University of Pennsylvania and Julie a junior at Yale. Both were scheduled to return to college in the fall. One day in early August, I was in Dutch's office when Marc came in and asked—pleaded—to take the semester off to work on the campaign.

"I know you can win, Dad, and I want to be here," he said.

Dutch responded a little too enthusiastically for my taste: "Your leaving now would be a great loss. You work like a Trojan. I don't know who can replace you."

"You can't interrupt your college education!" I protested. All over the country, students were dropping out of college temporarily to pursue one passion or another, and some never returned. "This is not a good idea, Marc. This would mean that we would have to pay three college tuitions when Jacques enters college in two years. It would be a serious financial strain."

Reluctantly, Dutch gave in to my reasoning.

A few weeks later, I drove Marc to the airport, listening to him lament that he would miss such a great opportunity.

He had been in Philadelphia only three days when he called Dutch in his office, where I happened to be again. "Daddy, I have just made arrangements with my faculty advisor to take a semester off to do an independent study, for which I would get three semester hours' credit. I'll have the proposal complete and approved before the day is over."

I got on the phone: "Marc, three hours is not the fifteen that you normally get in a semester."

To which Marc replied, "I promise I will graduate with my class. The campaign experience is one I can never get in any classroom. You are making history. I know it; I have to be a part of it."

Three days later, he was back on the job at Morial campaign headquarters. Jacques, who was in high school, volunteered to corral some friends to pass out fliers before all of the Saints football games in the Superdome. Cheri and Monique would come with me. And Julie, whose calling was medicine, would stay in school at Yale until the general election—if Dutch made it that far.

Eleven candidates entered the primary, which was open to all political parties and to independents. In the 1970s, there was a surge in black political organizations, including some with tremendous influence. Several had supported and endorsed white candidates. Dutch could not count on blanket endorsements from black organizations, even though black pride was running high. Some black leaders feared they would "waste" black votes and wind up with a mayor with no regard for their interests. Two white candidates, State Senator Nat Kiefer and State Representative deLesseps "Tony" Morrison, had the support and endorsement of several local African American political organizations, though not all.

"I will take my message directly to the people," Dutch told them. "I do not need an intermediary to talk to my people."

Because Dutch had grounding in the community and had been involved in the NAACP, the Urban League, and other civil rights groups, I encouraged him to do it his way. He targeted places where he had helped uplift black and poor neighborhoods. He went to churches, organizations, neighborhoods, community centers, clubs, bars, barbershops, and the homes of ordinary people. He had a natural ease with almost anyone. They could shake his hand, embrace him, and ask their own questions. I accompanied him into many communities. He covered much of the city.

Fortunately, Dutch also had a white following from the days of the Civil Rights Movement and his time as judge and legislator. Many knew of his work in the community; some were fellow members of organizations to which he belonged and had served on committees with him. They, too, held gatherings in their homes to acquaint their friends with Dutch's plans.

I called many of my friends and community contacts, asking them to host meetings and introduce Dutch to their friends and neighbors. Many of them were loyal and dedicated campaigners who spent long hours in the effort. I also involved myself in fundraising, which I had often done for organizations I supported. Follow-up for these events was done by volunteers of all ages, from senior citizens to teenagers who came to campaign headquarters after school or on Saturdays. The primary campaign was grueling and exhilarating at the same time. As the momentum built, so did our support.

On primary day, we gathered at the Saxony Ballroom on Canal Street and Claiborne Avenue. Many campaign workers came directly from the polls, a fourteen-hour day behind them. The returns began to come in about nine that night. People watched television screens at opposite ends of the room.

"We are going to make it to the general election!" someone shouted.

Still, nothing was official. At about ten-thirty, it was announced on television that Dutch would be in the general election with Nat Kiefer. The crowd broke into shouting and clapping and began singing "We Shall Overcome." Dutch took the microphone and proclaimed, "This is our win, a victory for all of us. Now, we must gear up for final victory."

Two days later, the official count showed that Councilman-at-Large Joseph DiRosa, who had beaten Dutch when he ran for city council, not Nat Kiefer, had claimed the second spot in the primary. The runoff was six weeks away. After that we'd be off and running again.

All staff and volunteers were committed to six more weeks of intense campaigning for the general election. The prospect of making history fueled people's passion, and new supporters piled on board. Our entire family gave every minute we could; we went to rallies and town-hall meetings.

In November, Julie came home from Yale for election weekend.

Throughout the campaign, we had heard no word from the appellate court. Then, ten days before the election, the United States Court of Appeals, sitting *en banc* (all nine judges, rather than the usual three), announced that the appeal was denied. Dutch could not retain his judicial seat if he lost the election. By then, we were in the homestretch, and there was no turning back.

On November 12, Election Day, Dutch was up and out before five in the morning. If the primary election was frenzied, the general election was filled with an electric excitement and passion. Campaign headquarters was a beehive of activity, as were satellite headquarters in several key neighborhoods. As reports came in that Dutch was doing well, we went home to freshen up.

At seven that night, we joined campaign leaders and strategists at the Hilton Hotel. Dutch's pollster, Ed Renwick, was among them. Ed had selected a representative number of voting precincts that reflected the demographics of the city. He determined that if Dutch won in those precincts, he would be victorious citywide. All evening, Ed was on the phone in the suite, taking calls from campaigners in the selected precincts. At about nine, just an hour after the polls closed, I overheard Ed whisper to Dutch, "Congratulations! You have it. You are the new mayor of New Orleans."

As Ed announced it to everyone in the suite, Dutch hugged me and the children. Shouts of joy erupted around us. Taking the freight elevator to avoid the crowds, we went downstairs to the ballroom. The cheering was thunderous as the election was called on television.

Dutch gave his victory speech, pledging to represent the entire city and to govern with an even hand and with intelligence, integrity, and sincerity. We left the stage to mingle with the crowd. Everyone wanted to embrace Dutch, to shake his hand, to touch him. We walked through the crushing crowd in the ballroom to greet our supporters. At some point,

Jacques and Julie, Dutch and Marc, Cheri and me, with Monique peeking in front of me on victory night
BRYAN BERTEAUX, PHOTOGRAPHER

the crowd was so dense I was lifted off the floor.

Seventy-six percent of African Americans had turned out to vote, and Dutch received 97 percent of that vote, plus 20 percent of the white vote. Now, Dutch was mayor-elect, but he would not be inaugurated until the first Monday in May 1978. This would offer ample time for a careful and thoughtful transition, so he and his staff could hit the ground running. He established a transition team and many task forces to address the issues he ran on. The task forces were peopled with experts in their fields, as well as ordinary citizens who had been advocates of the issues being addressed.

There was also a slight downside to the long interval between election and inauguration. Dutch was now unemployed. We were both worried, but it was not long before the Kennedy School of Government at Harvard University offered him a fellowship for the spring semester. He could commute to Cambridge, Massachusetts, for a couple of days and spend the rest of the week in New Orleans leading the transition. In addition, he was an adjunct professor at the University of New Orleans during the spring semester. Both positions provided some income.

We both breathed a sigh of relief. Although it was a rigorous schedule, Dutch was gifted with much energy and drive. He was genuinely excited about the future. In Boston, he was close enough to visit Julie in nearby New Haven, at Yale. Cheri, Monique, and I also visited him in Cambridge for a long weekend and saw him in action at the Kennedy School, engaged in a spirited panel discussion with two of his fellow mayors in front of a class of students.

The victory marked the end of a period of frenetic activity for me. When asked on election night what my plans were now that we had won, I said, "I am not programmed past tonight!" I had been juggling my job at Xavier University, my family, and the campaign, and I hadn't really come up for breath. I could now focus more closely on my new positions as director of special services at Xavier and—this one I hadn't figured out—first lady of New Orleans.

I was allowed to do no more than look through the bars of the fence. I have never forgotten those bars.

Ernest N. Morial

CHAPTER 19

New Orleans in Color

On the first Monday of May 1978, Dutch and I, along with seven councilmen and their wives, sat high on a platform in front of city hall, looking over the crowd of well-wishers. Some were sitting, some standing—there were so many they spilled onto Duncan Plaza. The sound system reverberated as Dr. Albert Dent, president of Dillard University, introduced Dutch.

He stood to deliver his inaugural address as the first African-American mayor of New Orleans. The bright Louisiana sun shone on the noonday event, but a breeze tempered the heat. I squinted into the sunlight. Then, to better concentrate as Dutch began to speak, I closed my eyes against the glare. He talked about his journey to this place and about his hopes:

> Many years ago when I was a small boy, I daily passed a beautiful park near Elysian Fields Avenue. Children were always playing there in a kind of freedom that came to them naturally. But because of the laws

of my childhood, I was allowed to do no more than look through the bars of the fence. I have never forgotten those bars. They stand forever in my memory as a symbol of a city divided against itself. They are the vital roots of my lifelong preoccupation with trying to bring people together.

As I sat listening, I was overwhelmed by the change that had come over the course of three decades. A black man who once could not step inside a public park because of his race was now at the helm of his city's government. The road to this place was long and arduous, gained one step at a time. Those steps were not just his—or ours. Many people and organizations had played a part. Each individual who had cast a vote for Dutch could truly call this their victory. For a moment, I wondered if their expectations might be so ethereal that any progress Dutch's administration might achieve would be minimal in their eyes. But Dutch's words pushed those thoughts away:

> I love this city of my birth and of my heritage. I am a product of its past and a symbol of hope for the future, of the old ways of discrimination and disappointment and of the new time of advancement and achievement. You now give me the opportunity to contribute to the future well being of this great city, a city like no other, full of the richness of life, of diversity and charm. But [it is] also a city full of despair and poverty for thousands and thousands of its citizens. If I am able to accomplish anything as your mayor, it would be to lessen that despair and to open the door to socio-economic advancement to the less fortunate among us.

With my eyes still closed against the sun, I considered that Dutch always had compassion for people in need, people who were often ignored by society. This would be a major focus of his administration. I knew he had developed plans during the transition process, but I was not yet privy to them. Still, I knew what would be at the heart of those plans even before he continued to speak:

> Ours will be an administration that embraces the ideal of the brotherhood of man. That has always been my creed. In this spirit, our administration will be dedicated to the inalienable rights of all citizens to equitable city services, be they white or black, rich or poor, or of any of the diverse nationalities which are now giving the rich tapestry of our culture new meaning and new strength.
>
> We will do so because we have learned so painfully that if arm-in-arm we cannot go forward together, then alienated and divided we will, most assuredly, go backward at a cost beyond measure, there to contemplate the waste in human lives, the shattered dreams and withered hopes with which we have become all too familiar. We must not ask our children to pay this terrible price . . . ever again.

Applause rang out throughout his address, but at this, people stood to their feet. I wanted to shout, *Amen!* I knew Dutch's fight on the civil rights battlefield and his daring to take on seemingly futile challenges had molded his resolve and sharpened his determination. I thought, *If only we can get it right.*

> Now, new vitality is emerging and reinforcing this greatest of all American traditions. Now, in constructive racial and ethnic communion, the economic salvation which has been the unfulfilled heritage of this city for more than 100 years is within our reach. This time it will not escape us. Ours will not be a government of one man, but of all men and all women. It will be neither a black administration nor a white administration. It belongs to no ethnic group. It will be an administration of all the people and it will be founded on integrity, intelligence, courage and the willingness to serve others well.

I cheered him silently and prayed he could make his dream a reality. The noonday sun had begun to retreat to the west of the gathering of people, but still my eyes were closed. I was thinking about myself now. I was excited to be part of the realization of these noble goals, but at the same time, I wondered what role I would play. Would I serve as a sounding board for Dutch as I had throughout his career, or would I do more? What would "more" be? I would have to be ready for any opportunity that surfaced. Dutch knew my special interests—the arts, children, education, women's issues. There would be a place for me.

But what sacrifices would our family have to make as Dutch kept his promises to his constituency? How would living in a fishbowl affect our children? They all were fairly well grounded, but would they remain that way? I knew I would be doing a lot of praying for Dutch and for our children. I was praying now. I squeezed my eyes more tightly closed and prayed to God to guide him and give him the strength and tenacity to fulfill his vision.

Dutch closed with the Louis Untermeyer poem "Prayer." It was something he always recited as he took on a new challenge. It meant so much to him, was such a part of him.

> GOD, though this life is but a wraith,
> Although we know not what we use,
> Although we grope with little faith,
> Give me the heart to fight—and lose.
>
> Ever insurgent let me be,
> Make me more daring than devout;
> From sleek contentment keep me free,
> And fill me with a buoyant doubt.
>
> Open my eyes to visions girt
> With beauty, and with wonder lit—

But always let me see the dirt,
And all that spawn and die in it.

Open my ears to music; let
Me thrill with Spring's first flutes and drums—
But never let me dare forget
The bitter ballads of the slums.

From compromise and things half done,
Keep me with stern and stubborn pride;
And when at last the fight is won,
God, keep me still unsatisfied.

The challenge now was governing and addressing the problems
Dutch had talked about on the campaign trail: jobs and economic development. New Orleans in some ways had been cut off, as many urban
areas had. Federal monies, including antipoverty funding, which President
Johnson had initiated, were drying up. Crime and public safety had been
issues for New Orleans for years. Added to this daunting mix was Dutch's
identity as one of the first black mayors of a Southern city. Together, it
was all more than intimidating.

Still, if I wasn't ready for Dutch to be mayor, he was. The long transition between his election on November 12, 1977, and this day in May—a
transition aided by the hundreds of citizens who participated—enabled
him to hit the ground running. His task-force format attracted many people from the private sector, both young and old, who were thrilled to offer their talents and perspectives to fashioning the Morial administration.
Quite a few of them decided to apply for permanent positions. Drawing
from professionals, transition participants (including grass-roots people
whose voices Dutch wanted to hear), and a few urban design students
with whom he had worked during his fellowship at Harvard's Kennedy
School, Dutch assembled a strong staff by Inauguration Day.

Governing structures were thought out carefully; that was one of Dutch's strong suits. He had a powerful executive team that included Anthony Mumphrey, Reynaud Rochon, James Chubbuck, Arnold Broussard, and executive counsel David Marcello. A list of department heads skilled in their fields joined the roster, ignited by Dutch's vision for New Orleans. That vision was a broad one, even for a mayor of a major metropolitan area. The social, economic, and physical facets of the city would be covered by an administration fully integrated—blacks, whites, women, and other minorities. Talented and highly qualified people, including neighborhood activists, were appointed to boards and commissions. Some were attracted to public service for the first time.

Dutch was nothing if not a hard worker. He was a strict taskmaster; poor performance was not acceptable. He set an example of commitment and competence, often reminding his staff, as he did our children, "You can't hoot with the owls and soar with the eagles." Or alternately, "You can't run with the foxes and sleep with the hounds."

He knew that crime and public safety—as well as police brutality—had to be addressed immediately. A new police chief would be critical in planning a strategy and implementing it. The person would have to both win over the police department and gain the trust of citizens.

I was busy preparing breakfast one morning as he pored over some notes about that issue. I had my mind on the grapefruit I was scoring when he started in on his plan: "Rather than searching and selecting a police chief myself, I could appoint a committee of citizens and ask them to conduct a national search."

I paused in my fruit cutting for a moment. I thought what he proposed was pretty much a win-win approach, but I had one deep reservation: "You'll get criticized if you cede your authority to a committee."

"But I'm not going to do that," he said, shaking his head. "I'll make the choice from their three finalists."

When he presented this novel approach, he received praise; the expected criticism was negligible. The Police Chief Selection Committee was formed of some thirty members, chaired by Xavier University president Norman Francis, a friend whom Dutch had consulted many times during his career. After a couple of months of intense searching, the committee handed over the names of three candidates. After in-depth interviews of all three, Dutch selected a white man, James Parsons from Birmingham, Alabama. On the surface, it was a strange selection. Parsons had been a member of the rank and file of Bull Connor's Birmingham police force during the brutal reaction to the Civil Rights Movement's campaign there. Although this gave Dutch pause, he felt comfortable with Parsons. Parsons had passed muster with the diverse search committee, and Dutch was impressed with his progressive views of making the New Orleans Police Department more professional and accountable.

Nevertheless, during Dutch's first year in office, a major crisis involving the police department would challenge his administration. It happened at the worst possible time, during New Orleans' most lavish and famous festival, Mardi Gras.

The Mardi Gras season begins on Twelfth Night, January 6, the date of the Epiphany, when the Magi visited Jesus. Private balls and colorful parties initiate the celebration. King cake parties are thrown throughout the city by every social class. The cake, a frosted brioche ring with a plastic baby baked inside, is divided among the revelers. The person who receives the baby in his or her slice must host the next king cake party. The parades begin ten days before the actual event of Mardi Gras ("Fat Tuesday" in French), which precedes the Lenten fast beginning on Ash Wednesday.

I grew up loving the rituals of Mardi Gras. The festival, of course, is New Orleans' signature event. Tourism and business depend on its success, and people look forward to it all year long. Revolving around Mardi Gras is a multifaceted industry: float designers and builders, *modistes* and seamstresses, caterers and party planners. That's not to mention bakers of king cakes and makers of masks and costumes. Then, of course, there are the retailers and wholesalers who sell every level of Mardi Gras merchandise, right down to the hundreds of thousands of parade trinkets, or "throws."

In the years before Dutch was mayor, our family had its own Mardi Gras ritual. Typically, we woke early and had a light breakfast. All five children would dress, sometimes in costume. If everything went smoothly, we were on our way to the home of Memere, Dutch's mother, by nine. She would make *calas*, special Creole rice fritters traditionally served at Mardi Gras time. Afterward, we would go to view the parades. When Dutch was a judge or in the legislature, we could watch from the stands reserved for elected officials. While he was mayor, we viewed the parades from the stands erected in front of Gallier Hall, formerly city hall. From there, as the floats and bands passed, he would toast the parade kings. The stands provided a bird's-eye view of the strolling maskers, marching clubs, and other revelers.

There are quite a number of parades. Some are old and traditional, among them Rex, Zulu, Hermes, and Babylon. Others—Endymion, Bacchus, Orpheus, and Muses (with an all-woman krewe)—are more recent additions.

The Zulu Club, originally an all-Negro parading group named for the South African Zulu tribe, dates back to 1909. For many years, it paraded only in Negro neighborhoods on flatbed carts with simple decorations. After the social upheaval of the 1960s, the Zulu Club upgraded its floats to compete with other parades and became one of the most popular parades on Mardi Gras day. It is followed by the parade of Rex, king of the carnival. Then comes the Truck Parade, featuring as many as three hundred truck floats decorated by private groups and clubs.

On Mardi Gras day, parades begin around nine in the morning and often last beyond three in the afternoon. The entertainment is sponsored by private groups, or "krewes," organized specifically for the yearly parades.

The mood is merry, and the crowds are thick on the parade routes. As the floats pass by, the viewers shout, "Throw me something, mister!" (Now, with women riding, they leave off the "mister.") The riders throw beads, trinkets, small toys—sometimes unique to that krewe—to the spectators. These make happy souvenirs for the natives, as well as tourists. Watching the lust for tossed treasures, the way the viewers scramble to catch them, one would think the throws were hundred-dollar bills. Bragging rights are in order for those whose catch is large.

The New Orleans Police Department does an extraordinary job at Mardi Gras time. Hundreds of thousands of happy—and sometimes intoxicated—revelers are treated with discretion. Aggressive discipline would interfere with the overall good nature of the festival, yet the police must maintain some sense of order and safety. New Orleans police are masters at crowd control. While other parades (such as New York's St. Patrick's Day and Macy's Thanksgiving parades) may get as many spectators, our parades go on for days and stretch for miles on their routes throughout the city. Crowds swell as Mardi Gras day gets closer. Visitors often marvel at the order among the seeming chaos.

Complementing the skills of the NOPD during this season is the city's sanitation department, which goes to work immediately after the parades. Huge trucks follow the floats, sweeping and picking up the considerable trash discarded by revelers. Remarkably, these industrious workers leave clean streets in their wake for the next day, Ash Wednesday, when the mood of yesterday's revelers makes a 180-degree turn. Without the skills of the police department and the services of the sanitation department, Mardi Gras would be impossibly chaotic.

The Police Association of New Orleans (PANO) was established as a union in 1969 and became affiliated with the Teamsters in 1978. Now, a year later, it was demanding a collective bargaining contract with the city of New Orleans.

The talk on the street was that if the city did not agree with the union's demands, the police would stage a job action. Radio talk shows buzzed with reports about a potential police strike. Callers expressed opinions pro and con; this heightened the conversation and created tension in the public and private sectors. By choosing to strike at Mardi Gras, PANO was guaranteeing leverage for itself. A million visitors were expected. Without police presence, Mardi Gras would bring the city to its knees.

Needless to say, Dutch was under considerable pressure to grant PANO its collective-bargaining contract. He met with his staff and local and state elected officials. He also called in the captains of the krewes to discuss the threat. Collectively, they decided to cancel their parades if the police went on strike.

It was a heartrending decision for all of them. The krewes devote immense time, energy, and money to designing and constructing the floats, costuming their riders, and purchasing trinkets and doubloons to throw to the crowds. They work from one Mardi Gras to the next to create something more mesmerizing each year.

Still, the strike went forward and the parades were canceled, though the Mardi Gras balls went on as scheduled. There was a lot of anger in the community. Some blamed the mayor. Others turned on the police force for choosing that time to strike. Many merchants, of course, depended on Mardi Gras for their livelihoods.

On the day before the strike began, I received a phone call at work from Police Chief Parsons. He said he wanted to come see me.

I was startled. "Has something happened to my husband?"

"No, I just need to share some information with you about security for you and your children at this time."

I could feel my heart begin to race. "I'd rather meet you at my home," I said. "I can be home in eight minutes. You can meet me there."

"Okay, just stay calm. I'll be right over."

This was not the first indication that our children might be at risk. In the fall, Julie, a junior at Yale, had received several disconcerting telephone calls from a stranger who wanted to meet her and take her out. He had seen her photo in a national magazine during the mayoral election. She called to tell us about it and was not particularly upset, but when the caller phoned to say he was in New Haven and wanted to see her, she really got frightened. She was baffled by how he got her phone number and feared he might know the residential college where she lived. A member of Dutch's staff began an investigation with campus security and the New Haven Police Department. We told Julie that the police were on alert, and to contact us if the man made any more contact. Through several investigations, we learned that he did not live in New Haven and was not a Yale student. He had been identified as someone with mental problems, and eventually the police apprehended him. That scare was over. Now, we faced another.

My drive home was tense. Eight minutes seemed like an hour. Police Chief Parsons and another officer arrived almost immediately. I escorted them into the den. It was a comfortable room, and I needed a close and safe place to hear whatever hard news they had to tell.

His officer continued to stand while Parsons sat. The chief said that because of the imminent strike, our family might not be safe. We needed to take some precautions. He made it clear that he didn't expect anything untoward to occur, but we needed to prepare just in case. He asked for my blood type and those of the children—a shocking first question— then asked which was our hospital of choice. I could feel my face flush, and he must have seen it, too. He immediately suggested that Charity Hospital had the best trauma unit in the city.

While we talked, the other officer took notes of our discussion. It seemed to me in my frightened state that Parsons wanted to know everything. I blinked hard when he asked for photos and Social Security numbers of the children. He asked the names of their schools, their arrival and departure times, how they got home each day. The other officer went out to his car and came back with several fire extinguishers. As a "precaution," he showed me how to activate them.

Chief Parsons then told me that a National Guard unit would be assigned to the premises to protect us. As I sat trying to absorb all this, the chief asked if I had any questions. Then he gave me a telephone number at which I could immediately reach him during this crisis.

When the children came home, I got the three of them together in the den and told them what was happening. The news wasn't a complete surprise. The pending strike had dominated the news, and no doubt they had heard Dutch and me discussing it. They were tense, though; I could see it in their faces.

The following day, the strike began. Early that morning, before I left to go to work, an officer wearing olive drab and boots rang our doorbell. He greeted me, identified himself as a member of the National Guard, apologized for the intrusion, and informed me that his unit was here to protect us. He asked for the key to the double gates leading to the backyard. "We will back our truck into your yard and stay until we get orders to leave," he said. "We will not need anything from you. We are self-contained and will not intrude on your lives."

I found this a bit ironic, as it was something of an intrusion to have a National Guard unit in our yard. He ended by saying that the men were here only for our protection. I watched as one of the guards began a continuous walk around the perimeter of the property.

By the time the children came home, the National Guard was entrenched in our yard, and a manned, marked police car was parked in front of our house.

During the strike, Dutch was at city hall sometimes as long as sixteen hours a day. Louisiana state troopers and the Louisiana National Guard arrived to replace striking police officers. A federal mediator was called in to help resolve the conflict.

Two days into the strike, I found out that our children were being taunted at school because their father had "canceled" Mardi Gras. Cheri's friends remained close, but other students whispered around her. The next day, I got a call at work from the girls' school principal. She said a man had called the school and claimed that he was going to take care of those Morial "brats." (The word may have been worse, but I suspected the nun wouldn't repeat it.) The call had come near the end of the school day. The principal said that the person seemed to know the school's layout, because he referred to specific interior locations. This frightened me.

The principal asked me what she should do, and I told her I would call back in a few minutes. When I got off the phone, I suppressed the immediate urge to call Dutch. He already had his hands full and didn't need to be further stressed. Instead, I called the police officer assigned to us, the one who had come to the house with Chief Parsons. As we discussed options to protect the children, I tried to stifle my panic. He insisted that we would get whatever help and support we needed. What ran through my mind, though, was that marked police cars and a bomb squad might cause panic at the school.

We decided instead to send over an unmarked police car manned by two officers to park in front of the school. The bomb squad would be put on alert.

By that time, I was a recognizable person in New Orleans; if I went to the school myself, there was little chance I could pass unnoticed. With grave doubts, I decided to let the girls come home with their usual carpool.

I raced home from work—my heart pounding—to be there when they arrived. I was panting as I came through the door. My daughters had arrived safely, and Jacques came in shortly afterward, having ridden the city bus. Mable Chantlan, our capable and loyal housekeeper, was there, too, standing guard.

My younger son, Jacques, just sixteen, kept his own counsel at that time. During the strike, I asked him several times if he was having any difficulty.

"Nothing I can't handle," he said.

Long after the strike, though, I learned that he was taunted daily. To avoid confrontation after school, he took different routes home every day, walking some days and taking the bus others. One day a week, he took a course at the University of New Orleans, so he left school early that afternoon. Later, he figured out that if he could make it to the public bus, the passengers would protect him.

The children coped with the situation in their individual ways. During the National Guard occupation, Monique, who was eight, played cards with the policewomen who staffed the marked car in front of our house. She also stood on our balcony facing the backyard where the National Guardsmen were and, pretending to be on a float, threw trinkets to them. She made the most of a stressful situation.

On Mardi Gras day, our house was pelted with onions, fish heads, and eggs. I sent my children to the home of my brother C. C. and his wife, Iris, for the day so they would not have that particular memory. Months later, while gardening, I found a stray onion in the yard.

At city hall, discussions between the city and PANO, assisted by the federal mediator, seemed to go on forever. Dutch came home each night totally exhausted. We barely exchanged words before he fell asleep.

After a sixteen-day strike no contract was signed, but Dutch finally restored a positive relationship between the city and the police department. Pay and benefits improved for police officers. They received better training, and the number of blacks hired as officers grew. New volunteer programs including Neighborhood Watch and Taxis on Patrol contributed to a decrease in crime.

Dutch continued to promote his vision for the city and to motivate the fine talents who served his administration. One new policy was the practice of "set-asides," which reserved 15 percent of city contracts for minorities and women. This was a real breakthrough. The Women's Business Enterprise Unit worked alongside the Office of Minority Business

Development and the Citywide Economic Development Corporation to bring women and minorities into the economic mainstream.

Dutch also brought new attention to the arts, which he called "New Orleans' treasure." I had served on various arts boards, including the New Orleans Council of the Arts for Children, New Orleans Young Audiences, and the New Orleans Ballet Association. He was especially interested in the visual arts. One evening as I was clearing the table after a late dinner, I asked what he was planning to do about the arts. "Don't put them at the bottom on your list of priorities," I said.

"No, I have been thinking about that a lot lately. I would like to see the city involved in the arts in some way. Maybe there is a role the city can play in bringing artists, various arts institutions and organizations, and policy experts to the table to talk about this. You can help with this. You know and have worked with many of the people we should involve."

I told him it was a great idea and that I was excited to help lead the effort.

Shortly thereafter, he established the Mayor's Task Force on Arts Policy. He appointed me co-chair and named people from all facets of the arts community to serve. He charged us to recommend to him the role the city should play in promoting the arts.

After several months of deliberating, the task force advised merging the private arts council with the city's to form the New Orleans Arts Council. This combined council, in turn, recommended public funding for art in public places, the establishment of the Municipal Endowment Fund to offer grants for arts projects beneficial to the community, and the establishment of the Mayor's Arts Awards to recognize local artists. Dutch accepted these recommendations and included funding for them in his budget.

Dutch always advocated for people with little voice in their destiny. He worked tirelessly to establish economic development that created jobs, neighborhood revitalization, safety, and new homes for low-income families. To give the voiceless access to power, he organized several strong initiatives including New Orleans Artists against Hunger and Homelessness; the Citizens Action Center, to assist people's access to city government; the Alliance for Human Services, to coordinate private and public efforts; the Fair Housing Unit; and the Mayor's Task Force on Nutrition.

All this did not go unnoticed in Washington. In the spring of 1980, we received another White House invitation. This time, President Jimmy Carter and his wife, Rosalynn, invited us to lunch.

We went on a beautiful day in early May, when blooming flowers blanketed the White House grounds. Once again, we arrived at the East Entrance, where we were escorted into a room with several wingback chairs, tables, and lamps. I noticed we were in a small group and whispered to Dutch, "Do you think this is it?"

"Shh," he replied.

We were guided to an elevator that took us up a level. When the door opened, we walked into the president's private living quarters! Among the twelve of us guests were two other mayors and their spouses, two governors and their spouses, and a cabinet member and his spouse. The president and the first lady warmly greeted us.

The Carters were seated opposite each other in the middle of a rectangular table (as the president traditionally sits in cabinet meetings). The rest of us were seated around them. The conversation was informal, the president drawing out comments from his guests. First Lady Rosalynn was very involved in the conversation. There did not seem to be an agenda.

Our meal was a New England seafood dish with baby vegetables and an elegant fruit tart for dessert. The casual and warm event was quite different from the formal state dinner we had attended some ten years earlier. Afterward, we were given a tour of the first family's residence, including the room of the Carters' daughter, Amy, who was nine just like

*Dutch and I share a kiss after his second inauguration as mayor of New
Orleans, 1982. Judge Steven Plotkin and Judge Revius Ortique officiate.*
AUTHOR'S COLLECTION

our youngest daughter, had a Hula-Hoop just like Monique's.

In 1980, Ronald Reagan beat Jimmy Carter in his bid for a second
term. Dutch's second-term victory allowed him to continue the initiatives begun in his first term, many of which came to fruition during the
following years.

I bathed in the Euphrates when dawns were
young.
I built my hut near the Congo and it lulled
me to sleep.
I looked upon the Nile and raised the pyra-
mids above it.
I heard the singing of the Mississippi when
Abe Lincoln went down to New Orleans,
and I've seen its muddy bosom turn all
golden in the sunset.

I've known rivers:
Ancient, dusky rivers.

My soul has grown deep like the rivers.

Langston Hughes

CHAPTER 20

I've Known Rivers

A hundred years after the first cotton left the New World for the Old, New Orleans held a celebration in honor of that trade. It happened in 1884 and was known as the World's Industrial and Cotton Centennial. Another hundred years passed, and in the midst of another World's Fair in New Orleans, we managed to honor some of the voices, labor, and arts of the people whose ancestors had picked and baled and threshed and woven that cotton.

The first event, the Cotton Centennial, had in a small way honored the Negro. According to scholar Ruth Winston, the exhibit had a special section supported by a substantial investment for that time: fifty thousand dollars. The Negro exhibit in 1884 occupied a gallery at the north end of a government building. The work displayed was mainly that of women—embroidery, sewing, and household stuffs. Some crafts done by artisans were presented, together with work sent by Negro schools to display the progress Negro education was making. On Louisiana Day, Negro men and women walked in the parade and participated in the ceremonies. A minister spoke of hope for progress.

The Cotton Centennial was held on the site of what is now Audubon Park. Our exposition in 1984 would be a larger event and would be spread out along the Mississippi River in the deteriorating Warehouse District. The fair would provide a growth opportunity for New Orleans, a city suffering from a drought of federal funding since President Johnson's War on Poverty funds had evaporated. We needed new buildings and area development to promote tourism, business, and conventions. The city had never had difficulty bringing in people for Mardi Gras, but it needed a broader base for visitors.

The exposition seemed a great opportunity to do this. First of all, World's Fairs attracted people from all over the globe. Such events provided the opportunity for the host cities to showcase their resources, culture, and talent, of which New Orleans had an excess. After the fairs were over, they provided residuals—buildings and other structures—that broadened cities' economic bases. In New Orleans, the fair would revitalize the Warehouse District and help create the Riverwalk Mall, which would roll along the edge of the Mississippi crescent that defines the city.

The design for the fair gradually took shape. Some stunning exhibits were planned. NASA offered to display the *Discovery* space shuttle. The Vatican would contribute an exhibit of its artwork. Countries from Europe, Asia, and Africa would have pavilions at the fair. We also wanted to present food, art, and entertainment that were distinctively New Orleans.

Many things had changed in the city by the time we embarked on our World's Fair journey. For one thing, a black man, who happened to be my husband, had been elected to the office of mayor. Dutch had recently embarked on a second term. We wanted an exhibit at the fair that spoke to the African American presence in New Orleans and the United States.

A cogent idea for the Afro-American Pavilion at the fair grew out of a conversation with my Xavier University colleague and friend John Scott. Shortly before Dutch was elected to a second term as mayor, John and I were musing over lunch in the faculty dining room, as we often did, about the obscured history of black people.

In addition to being a nationally renowned sculptor, John taught art at Xavier. As we talked about the Louisiana World Exposition, as the planned fair was to be called, we came up with the same thought: the majority black population in New Orleans mandated an African American presence at the fair. Such an exhibit would provide an excellent stage for sharing the contributions that black people had made throughout American history. On television only five years before, Alex Haley's *Roots* had reminded a large national audience of our African heritage. Still, little national focus had followed on the contributions of African Americans.

Our vision for the exhibit evolved over several tête-à-têtes. Finally, I said, "John, I am getting more and more excited. I am going to talk to Dutch about this."

That night, as soon as Dutch came home, I brought it up. My timing was not good. That afternoon, he had endured a particularly stressful discussion with Louisiana World Exposition, Inc., the organization responsible for organizing the fair. Nevertheless, he didn't shoot down my idea.

"I agree that it would be great to have a presence at the fair. Who would create it?"

"I don't know. Whoever does it, I would like to be involved."

He paused for a moment, then responded carefully, "The World's Fair is going to be an opportunity for christening the convention center, for getting it national attention. But I'm worried about the financial viability. The city cannot be at all responsible for any exhibit costs except utilities. Today, I made this clear with the organizers."

That was hard to accept. "Would the city be able to help us at all?"

Somehow, I knew this was a futile inquiry. Dutch immediately said no. The city could not underwrite it or be a sponsor in any way for this or any exhibit.

"If there was any hint that this would get any help from the city or me, I would have all sorts of requests for city support. I'm sorry. You would have to get some other sponsor to underwrite the exhibit."

The next day, I reported the bad news to John. We were disappoint ed, but our enthusiasm wasn't quelled. We decided to share our idea with others.

Through the next weeks, John and I talked up our idea among people we knew, but although there was enthusiasm, we found no takers. So we decided to initiate the project and hope a sponsor would surface. Our idea certainly did not lack naïveté! We decided that John would corral people to design the exhibition and I would organize community and financial support. When we shared the idea with Petr Spurney, the fair's president, he encouraged us but offered no financial support.

Our centennial would be much larger than the original Cotton Centennial celebration of Negro industry. With the help of friends, we identified sixty-two people and organizations we would ask for support. Alden McDonald, president of Liberty Bank and Trust Company, a mi- nority bank, offered in-kind support from his bank, which would be our mainstay. Later, Soft Sheen Beauty Products of Chicago would join as our major sponsor.

At the initial meeting of the potential sponsors, I talked about the importance of sharing black contributions to America and John talked about creating a design of which we could all be proud. We received unanimous pledges of support and enthusiasm, and the group became charter members of the Afro-American Pavilion. We had only twenty months to finance, design, and mount a major exposition. Privately, I was worried that we could not raise the money. What was I doing taking on this mammoth challenge? But we kept going.

John convened a group of artists, architects, and historians into a design team. In keeping with the theme of the Louisiana World Exposition, "Rivers of the World," we selected as our theme "I've Known Rivers" from the Langston Hughes poem "The Negro Speaks of Rivers." By then, I had visited Africa twice and was aware of how the continent is made up of large and small river cultures and how rivers were the main mode of transportation throughout much of Africa well into the twentieth century. And here we were in the state of Louisiana, sitting on the Mississippi, which had shaped the lives of so many people of color.

The exhibit graduated into a pavilion so we could expand the presentation. We plowed along, determined it would become a reality. Much of the help we received was pro bono. The initial group that pledged support became our cheering squad and campaign committee. Liberty Bank provided space for us to operate, and from that location we began in earnest

I'VE KNOWN RIVERS, INC.
Afro-American Pavilion
1984 Louisiana World Exposition

DESIGNED BY
JOHN SCOTT

THE

SPECTATOR

50¢

NEWS JOURNAL

Sybil Morial and Artist John Scott

of

I've Known Rivers Inc.

Sybil and John Scott with a model of the pavilion
SPECTATOR NEWS JOURNAL

to identify sources of financial support. First, we had to estimate how much we needed for the project. After a few weeks, the design team came up with a ballpark figure of $2 million. That staggering amount could not be raised in New Orleans, or in Louisiana alone. We had to go national in seeking support.

I knew that when we solicited funds from national corporations, they would want to know what support was expected from local businesses. At a hotel downtown, I arranged a meeting with top executives of eleven large local companies. Ten attended, and the eleventh invited me to meet with him in his office. I presented the "I've Known Rivers" plan and explained that I needed $250,000 from combined local businesses as leverage in raising money nationally. I asked for their collective support. The meeting ended with pledges up to $200,000.

I met with one last potential donor in a high-rise maritime building overlooking a port on the Mississippi. He welcomed me warmly. As I began to make the presentation, however, his telephone rang. He asked me to excuse him, as he had to take an international call. As I sat there, I could not help overhearing his side of the conversation: "I think $1 billion will do it," he said into the receiver. "We need not go higher. Make the offer."

The amount of money he had dispensed in seconds took my breath away. When he hung up, he apologized for the interruption, and I presented my case. I ended with this: "And I am only asking for $10,000!"

He laughed and said, "Touché, Mrs. Morial. You have it!"

At that time, several African Americans were serving on national corporate boards that might prove great contacts. We had a model of the pavilion made and took it on the road. On our journey, we were helped by dozens of people and organizations that offered in-kind support. Pan Am provided passes for transportation to New York and Chicago. Chauffeur and car service was provided by an anonymous donor in New York City.

A major challenge was securing ongoing funds to hire staff, because the effort became intense and required full-time people with expertise. To complement our new hires—Clifford Johnson as executive director and Quinta Martin as assistant executive director—we were able to secure an executive loan from a corporation in the city to bring its expertise to the project. We hired C. C. Campbell-Rock to generate publicity; my daughter Cheri assisted her.

John and I appeared on a number of local television shows. Besides local media, the pavilion was featured in magazines including *Ebony, Jet,* and *Black Enterprise.* We also had coverage on New York and Chicago radio and in airline publications.

On opening day, John and I, along with representatives of our major sponsors—Alden McDonald of Liberty Bank and Mr. and Mrs. Edward Gardner, owners of Soft Sheen—gathered with the design team, which included architects, historians, and artists. Together, we cut the ribbon to the pavilion amid much fanfare and many, many fans and supporters. As its major face and spokesperson, I was given the opportunity to welcome visitors to the exhibit via a video. Journalist Tony Brown loaned us wonderful historical films that he had aired on public television over the years on his weekly show, *Tony Brown's Journal.* They played constantly on eight monitors throughout the exhibit.

The Afro-American Pavilion was located in the main hall, what would become the first building of the convention center. Its facade was a huge rhomboid-shaped structure. Its stucco surface suggested the red clay of West Africa, where slaves had been captured and transported. It was also reminiscent of the red clay of the Southern farmlands where slaves had toiled. Brightly colored symbols of African American history coupled with continental African iconography in bas-relief covered the stucco.

The Afro-American Pavilion would concentrate on the contributions of African Americans to life in the United States, but we wanted people to realize that those contributions sprang from a history of anguish and affliction that was all too often discounted. We wanted to convey a brief token of the experience. So, in the center of the main hall in New Orleans' brand-new convention center, just blocks from Canal Street and alongside the Mississippi, we simulated the Middle Passage of Africans captured and brought to America in chains some two hundred years ago.

As visitors entered the pavilion, a message of welcome and a hint of what would come were presented on a television monitor. The door to the exhibit slid open, and about twenty people entered a space of just six by twelve feet. When the door closed, the lights dimmed, and the people standing elevator-close to each other heard the pounding of the ocean. A deep bass voice narrated the scene. Photos of Africans being carried as cargo appeared in succession high on the walls. Those human beings were stacked in shelves so tightly that they could not move. There were images of brutal beatings and other violations. The whole thing lasted about five minutes, but when the door slid open again, many of the people leaving were stunned, some in tears. Others were angry, thinking that the facts were exaggerated.

As visitors exited the Middle Passage, which was the beginning of the African presence in America, they faced a mural depicting slavery, a field with slaves bent over picking cotton. An overseer brandished a whip, and a slave cabin stood in the background. A student trained as a docent—Monique was one—met the group at this point and began a tour of the history and contributions black people had made to the United States since they were brought to this side of the Atlantic. As visitors moved along, those contributions unfolded in front of them. Narratives on TV monitors accompanied the presentations. An exhibit on arts and culture presented encased artifacts, including musical scores and literary pieces. A larger-than-life figure of Martin Luther King Jr. loomed over the civil rights exhibit. A huge figure of Mary McLeod Bethune, president of Bethune-Cookman College and a friend of Eleanor Roosevelt, presided over the education exhibit. The business exhibit featured a life-sized sculpture of a barber with a client in a barber chair. A giant replica of research scientist George Washington Carver welcomed visitors to the science exhibit. Mounted behind Carver was a list of United States–patented inventions by Negroes, forty-seven in all.

Amid many other attractions at the fair, the Afro-American Pavilion was constantly bustling with visitors, staff, and live music. A performance stage featured three shows a day. Opera, jazz, and blues performers, poets, actors, and dancers of all genres entertained visitors. Many national African American leaders—including Coretta Scott King, Andrew Young, Jesse Jackson, Alex Haley, *Black Enterprise* publisher Earl Graves, historian Lerone Bennett, Congressman Charles Rangel, and more—made appearances. Up a ramp to the mezzanine was a rotating exhibit of the work of noted African American artists including Jacob Lawrence and Elizabeth Catlett. A gift shop offered posters and other memorabilia. The millions who came to the exhibit were duly impressed. The fair established a precedent for New Orleans and provided an impetus for the transformation the city needed.

One of the major accomplishments of Dutch's tenure as mayor was securing and coordinating the funding for the convention center. Even though tourism had always been one of our largest industries, New Orleans did not have sufficient facilities for major conventions to make it competitive with other large cities. Dutch knew we had to have a real convention center. In his first term, he saw funding possibilities in a federal Urban Development Action Grant offered by the Carter administration that could be used to leverage local, state, and private funds to complete such a large project. And he was successful in guiding the multiple funding entities through the complex process. Several years after his death, the convention center was named in his honor, in recognition of his role in its initial development.

The exposition was also credited with revitalizing the Warehouse District and creating the Riverwalk. According to an early article in the *New York Times*, "The other major contemporary design ideas built into the Exposition include the adaptive reuse of old buildings (warehouses turned into an entertainment and restaurant district) and the interpretation of a working area of the city (in this case, the docks) as a place of leisure." The article ended, "For New Orleans, the legacy of the fair will be a recaptured riverfront, the stabilization of a warehouse district and an area that will be the framework for future development."

New Orleans' association with the history of black people did not end with the Afro-American Pavilion at the World's Fair. During his administration, Dutch, with the support of university presidents Norman Francis at Xavier and Eamon Kelly at Tulane, managed to fight off the relocation of the Amistad Research Center, the national historical archives of blacks and other minorities, located in New Orleans since 1970. It remains on the Tulane University campus and operates independently with an independent board.

Further progress was to come. During Dutch's second term, many of the initiatives established early in his administration hit their stride and flourished, and others came to fruition. Through the Women's Business Enterprise Unit and the Office of Minority Business Development, more women and minorities participated in public and private contracts than ever before. The latter organization became a model for other city governments around the nation. To attract new industries to New Orleans, Dutch also established the Almonaster-Michoud Industrial District, which featured access by rail, water, and interstate highway.

As a member of the steering committee, I welcomed John Paul II to New Orleans in 1987. It was the first visit to the city by any pope.
AUTHOR'S COLLECTION

With Prime Minister Margaret Thatcher and Phyllis Dennery at the British Embassy in Washington for reception of the board of the International Women's Forum (1988)
TIMES-PICAYUNE NEWSPAPER

Right: *With Andrew Young during the Super Bowl in New Orleans in 1997*
AUTHOR'S COLLECTION

Left: *Myrlie Evers and Sybil at the Martin Luther King Jr. Memorial Dedication*
AUTHOR'S COLLECTION

At the United States Embassy to the Holy See in Rome, at the canonization of Saint Katharine Drexel, founder of Xavier University. The reception was hosted by the ambassador to the Holy See, Lindy Boggs. Standing beside Sybil are Blanche Francis, Ambassador Boggs, Xavier University president Dr. Norman Francis, and Katherine Francis. AUTHOR'S COLLECTION

And knowing their thoughts Jesus said to them, "Any kingdom divided against itself is laid waste; and any city or house divided against itself will not stand."

Matthew 12:5

CHAPTER 21

A House Divided

"*I am an actor*, Mrs. Morial. I am not a news reporter."

The majestic voice of James Earl Jones boomed at me through the hot September air. He was standing on the median in front of the Woolworth's five-and-dime store where, twenty-five years earlier, students had staged sit-ins in order to integrate the lunch counter. It was a typically sweltering midafternoon on Canal Street, with streetcars clanging, horns blaring, and noisy crowds of shoppers. Mr. Jones, wearing a suit, was not happy.

The world of documentary filmmaking was new to both of us. This was definitely not one of the Shakespearean roles he was famous for; he was used to taking on a character, not reading from a monitor. But he was a consummate professional, and I knew he'd get it right.

I had come out the side door of university life to produce a work about desegregation in New Orleans, and I was just getting used to my own role. While working with students in a number of positions at Xavier University, I had discovered that many of them, both local and out-of-state, had some knowledge of the violence and brutality of the Civil Rights Movement. Many knew the cities that had made the television news— Birmingham, Selma, Montgomery, Atlanta, Memphis, and Jackson. But they had little or no idea of how New Orleans and its people had experienced resistance to integration and change. Nor did they understand how many landmark events had occurred in Louisiana. Even students native to New Orleans did not know that desegregation was ugly in this part of the South, too, and that resistance to it had been strong, although less violent than in other cities.

The documentary that I was producing and Jones was narrating aspired to remedy that. It was called *A House Divided*. His star was rapidly rising, and his presence and the depth of his commentary would lend luster to the project.

The documentary sprang from a concept created by Xavier's Drexel Center for Extended Learning, an institution designed to address the academic needs of working adults in the community. When I arrived at the center and took the position of associate dean, I found that Burwell Ware, who had been on the staff of the university's Department of Communications, was constructing short videos to be aired in prime time on public television. He was also shooting videos on living skills to be shown in the waiting rooms at welfare and employment offices and in public health clinics. Some of these addressed my students' prospects. And he was videotaping interviews with high-profile public and private individuals who were involved in both sides of the struggle over ending segregation in New Orleans' schools.

Since I had been involved with the Afro-American Pavilion at the 1984 World's Fair, I was particularly intrigued by Burwell's interviews with leaders and participants in the Civil Rights Movement. They could provide a remedy to students' ignorance of a segment of local history that was part of the bigger picture. We began to collaborate on a larger work and were able to interview Coretta Scott King, Andrew Young, Earl Graves, and Jesse Jackson, among others, some of whom had appeared at the pavilion.

It was also my job as executive producer to get the university's president, Norman Francis, to endorse and support the project, to find funding, and to secure the in-kind support we would need to complete the project. Burwell would produce the film, taping the subjects and using communications students for technical assistance. He would also secure news footage from television stations to put our interviews into broader context. With some help from me and other consultants, he would develop the ultimate story line.

Gathering from local stations news footage that sometimes showed graphic brutality was a challenge. Then we had to get permission to use it. The Reverend Avery Alexander, a prominent local activist, had been one of the people who sat-in at the cafeteria in the basement of city hall in 1963. His demeanor had been polite as he requested service, but he was refused and asked to leave. He was a large man, over six feet tall, and when he didn't comply, three policemen knocked him down, grabbed him by the feet, and dragged him up the concrete steps with his head bouncing on each one as they took him to the police car. It was a heart-wrenching scene that embarrassed the police department, and we knew it had been recorded and aired on the local news at least once. It took some serious effort to secure the original footage, but we found it at the BBC and included it.

Many activists and others provided commentary throughout the film. Andrew Young, who was then mayor of Atlanta, offered this about growing up in the city: "I would get thirsty downtown and wouldn't [be able] to get a drink of water. Or I'd look in the paper and [see] in City Park that there would be track meets and swimming meets and I could run and I could swim, but I couldn't [participate] in them. I didn't get beat up. I didn't get cussed at . . . but the subtleties of segregation, I think, probably did more damage than I realized."

The Reverend Alexander provided commentary in the present tense, telling about the casual violence that blacks had to endure:

> There was a wake. Now, blacks didn't have adequate funeral homes. When a person died, they brought the coffin or the casket, and they set it up in the front of the house and the friends came around. . . . And it would become a sort of social affair and people would stand around. And where they were standing out there, a white policemen [would] come by (there were no black police) and get out his gun and say, "Run, you niggers. Run." They used to do that all the time.
>
> There was one fellow who couldn't hear. He was just looking around; he didn't know what was going on. The policeman said, "When I tell you to run, you so-and-so, run. . . ." And he shot and killed him. Of course, people grieved and people said how terrible it was. And that was it; we couldn't even petition. If you said anything, you in turn would be arrested.

We included several other news clips and the opening scene from the movie *A Streetcar Named Desire*.

Our next challenge was editing the footage. By then, we had about a hundred hours of film, far more than we could use. The editing process took enormous amounts of time and required appropriate equipment. Local station WVUE, an ABC affiliate, was very supportive in providing consultation and the use of its facilities after hours to edit the footage and complete the documentary.

Now, we were in the homestretch. Once the documentary was ready to be packaged, it occurred to me that it could be used in the schools as a social studies or history unit. I engaged a Department of Education faculty member at Xavier, Sister Mary Loyola, to develop a teacher's guide, which she did with the assistance of several educators. With the guide

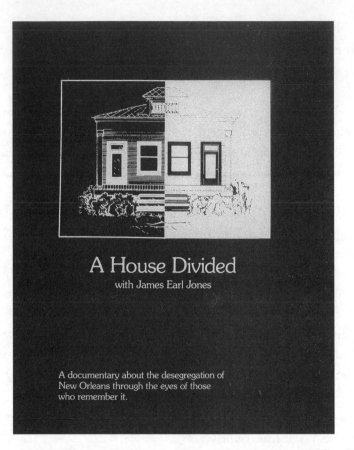

A House Divided
with James Earl Jones

A documentary about the desegregation of
New Orleans through the eyes of those
who remember it.

and hour-long video, we had a complete package that could be distributed to all public, parochial, and private schools and all branches of the New Orleans Public Library, as well as to colleges and universities in the area. And that is what we did.

A local hotel, Le Meridien, donated its facilities for the documentary's premiere, followed by a reception attended by many of the participants, interviewees, funders, supporters, faculty, staff, and students. Then WVUE aired the documentary in prime time.

A House Divided has aired consistently ever since its 1987 premiere, especially during Black History Month.

In the fell clutch of circumstance
I have not winced nor cried aloud.
Under the bludgeonings of chance
My head is bloody, but unbowed.

William Ernest Henley, "Invictus"

CHAPTER 22

Silence in the House

Friday, December 23, 1989, was bitterly cold. Despite an ice storm unlike any I had experienced, Dutch had taken Cheri and Monique shopping for last-minute Christmas gifts. Because they shopped in the mall, I didn't worry that he and the girls would be standing long in the horrid weather. I was at home preparing a Christmas Eve family dinner, a real New Orleans–style feast with gumbo, my grandmother's oyster dressing, and mirlitons, pear-like vegetables stuffed with seafood. All of these dishes are labor intensive, so I usually began a day early. I was in the midst of chopping seasonings and making a *roux* for the gumbo when Dutch called and asked if I needed anything.

"No, I don't think I forgot anything," I said absently.

Some hours later, he and the girls returned with faces rosy from the cold. They all remarked on the aromas of the food cooking—the gumbo smelled especially good—and asked if they could have a taste of the next day's meal.

"Yes, just a taste," I said.

After savoring a few bites, the girls wrapped the gifts they had bought and dressed to go to a party. Dutch went to his friend Jerry Glazer's house to watch a football game. I was relieved, after a long day of being on my feet, to have some time to be alone and to rest. I needed to be fresh in the morning to finish the cooking for the three o'clock meal. The girls would help me by setting the table and preparing a couple of accompanying dishes, as Jean and I had done for our mother when I was a teenager.

Julie was due to arrive at about ten that night from San Francisco, where she had begun working on a master's degree in public health at the nearby University of California, Berkeley. She had already completed her M.D. at the University of Pennsylvania and her residency at Northwestern University in Illinois. Marc and I had planned to go to the airport to pick her up, but just as I was freshening up, I got a cryptic telephone call from Jerry Glazer.

"Sybil, you need to go to Mercy Hospital."

"What's wrong? Is something wrong with Dutch?"

"Go to the ER. Just get there."

I could hear my heart pounding in my chest as Marc arrived. I immediately called my brother Glenn and asked him to go to the airport in my place to pick up Julie. I told him that he should bring Julie to the hospital, where Marc and I were now headed. Then I called Jacques and asked him to meet us there.

I was shaking as Marc parked the car at the hospital and we went up the ramp to the ER. One of Dutch's former security men appeared from nowhere, and I asked him to please go get Cheri and Monique, who were at their friend's party.

Sister Barbara, the hospital's administrator, took us to a private room, and Dutch's internist, Dr. Joseph Allain, joined Marc, Jacques, Sister Barbara, and me. By then, Julie, Cheri, and Monique had also arrived. Dr. Allain explained to all of us that he had been in the hospital coincidentally when Dutch was brought in unconscious. He said the staff was working still to resuscitate him.

Brad Glazer, Jerry's son, said that Dutch had bundled up to leave the warm, cozy room where they had watched the football game before heading out into the freezing cold to his car. About fifteen minutes later, a neighbor called and said she had seen a car with its lights on and a door ajar in the Glazer driveway. When the Glazers reached Dutch, he was unconscious. Jerry called 911 and then called me.

Dutch had asthma all his adult life. Although he took medication, his asthma was never severe. He had learned to avoid certain foods that caused minor distress and never let his asthma limit his fast-paced agenda. Sudden changes in temperature—not common in New Orleans— caused him to be short of breath, but he usually overcame it quickly and continued whatever he was doing. Not that day.

Very quickly, close friends who had heard about his attack arrived in the ER and were there to console us. I had never seen so many grown men crying, sobbing, and pacing up and down. Nevertheless, their presence comforted us.

Shortly after midnight, early on Christmas Eve, Dutch passed away. The cause of death was cardiac arrest, precipitated by an acute asthma attack. He had just turned sixty years old.

All five of the children came home with me from the hospital and sat on the floor around the lounge chair in my bedroom. We tried to fathom the reality of Dutch's death as we comforted each other. After a while, our conversation took a turn. We were not focusing on his death anymore but remembering his life, reminiscing about stories that made us laugh, each child relating a favorite memory, all recalling his warnings as the occasion dictated—"You can't hoot . . ." and "You can't run . . ." Before we knew it, we were reveling in his life, his joy of taking on challenges, his unbelievable work ethic, his love of dressing nattily, his purchases of clothes for me and all the children. He had been a creative cook and a neat and orderly person who insisted that a disciplined mind was necessary to achieve goals and get things done. Those memories eased our grief.

Our Christmas Eve dinner somehow slipped away. We agreed that we had to share Dutch's "going home" with those who had supported him. Despite tremendous odds, he had made history and affected the lives of many people who had long struggled for an identity and way of living. Before we knew it, with lifted spirits, we were planning his funeral as a celebration of his life.

In the wee hours of Christmas Day, all the children retired. After a few hours of rest, we met again to resume planning. Although Dutch had been out of public office for three years, his political family appeared in full force that morning to assist us. All we had to do was describe our wishes and they immediately went to work. Dutch was a stickler for details, so we knew his former staff would handle his funeral with great competence and care.

On Christmas Day, we were still numb from the shock of his death and weren't in the mood for the holiday. Our home was decorated for the joy of Christmas, but there was no joy in our house. Presents were under the tree, some from Dutch. Traditionally on Christmas morning, we sat around the tree and distributed gifts and opened them to oohs and aahs and bear hugs of thanks. Dutch always gave the children a surprise gift, in addition to what Santa Claus left. That day as we passed out presents, they were happy and tearful at the same time.

Later, we went to the home of my brother C. C. and his wife, Iris, for dinner with the extended family. Dutch and I and the children had done this yearly, since my parents no longer were able to host the gathering. Our first thought was to stay home and spend time together to help each other accept the reality of our tragedy. But C. C. suggested that we needed a break, so off we went to his home, less than a mile away.

Monsignor Roger Morin worked in Dutch's administration. I had collaborated with him as well when Pope John Paul II visited New Orleans. On Christmas Eve, Monsignor Morin graciously came to our home to help plan the funeral with our family. The service would be held at the St. Louis Cathedral-Basilica in three days. He promised to come back the day after Christmas to complete the plans.

Dutch's body would lie in state for one day at Gallier Hall, the old city hall, a grand building where many of the city's socials were held. On the evening before the funeral, a celebration of his life would be held in Municipal Auditorium, which Dutch had helped to integrate. It would be hosted by Judge Revius Ortique, with remembrances by United States senator J. Bennett Johnston; Democratic National Committee chairman Ron Brown; Congressman Ron Dellums, president of the Congressional Black Caucus; Tulane president Eamon Kelly; restaurateur and longtime friend and supporter Leah Chase; and NAACP president Benjamin Hooks. Moses Hogan, who had worked with me on many music programs for the city, planned the music for the funeral mass, which would include Aaron Neville's a cappella "Ave Maria." When the time arrived, we had a joyous evening celebrating Dutch's life with friends and supporters. More than ten thousand people paid their respects at Gallier Hall.

By the day of the funeral, though, I lost my grounding. The events passed in a blur. I went through the motions aware but not entirely there. Some closure came days later when I read about the funeral and saw a rerun of the televised events. It made the reality of losing Dutch final.

The funeral cortege left Gallier Hall and traveled past significant sites in Dutch's life, including city hall and the site of the Claver Building, which had housed the local NAACP and Dutch's first campaign headquarters; the structure itself no longer stood but had major significance during the Civil Rights Movement. Then we proceeded past the Lafitte Housing Project, where many of the people Dutch cared about lived, and then finally to Jackson Square and the cathedral. All along the route stood

In New Orleans tradition, second-liners march Dutch Morial to the grave site, December 1989.
TIMES-PICAYUNE NEWSPAPER

the people of New Orleans, some crying, others waving or making the sign of the cross. Some carried signs—"Thanks, Dutch" and "We Love You." This display of public affection was at once touching and consoling.

Inside the cathedral, Archbishop Philip Hannan, with whom Dutch and I had collaborated on church and city projects, gave the sermon.

Norman Francis, our longtime friend and confidant, gave a moving eulogy, opening with the poem "Invictus":

> Out of the night that covers me,
> Black as the pit from pole to pole,
> I thank whatever gods may be
> For my unconquerable soul. . . .

> It matters not how strait the gate,
> How charged with punishments the scroll,
> I am the master of my fate,
> I am the captain of my soul.

Then Marc spoke to us. His eulogy was direct and personal, expressing thanks to all the people who had made "this very difficult episode in our lives somewhat bearable." And he thanked both his father and me for "things that no one could ever take away." He paraphrased Kipling, expressing gratitude for learning "how to walk with kings and not lose the common touch, how to think without making thoughts your aim, and how to meet triumph and disaster and treat those two imposters just the same."

Finally, he made a plea for Dutch's legacy: "People asked me if he was arrogant. And I say, yes. He was arrogant. Because the times demanded it. The times required it. The times needed the competence, the spirit of Dutch."

Marc insisted that those present, including Dutch's children, needed that spirit to continue the work Dutch had begun: "I can say, Daddy, because I know you are still listening, that you have left five strong branches, five strong branches, and we can carry the load! We are going to keep the faith!"

The cathedral choir's music soared, and Wynton Marsalis performed

"Just a Closer Walk with Thee" on his trumpet. A traditional jazz funeral followed. After the funeral mass ended, friends and family followed the casket from the church, accompanied by the Olympia Brass Band, on the way to the cemetery a half-mile away. Playing mournful hymns and dirges, the band led the cortege. Throngs of people fell into step, forming the "second line," to the beat of the tuba.

After Dutch was laid to rest, the jazz band struck up joyful music to suggest his transfer to the next life. The second line, strutting to the up-beat "When the Saints Go Marching In," grew to a large number. One of the second liners was the singer Charmaine Neville, from one of the most famous musical families of New Orleans. She spoke about the meaning of the second line to a *Times-Picayune* reporter: "This was definitely the right way for Dutch to go out. Second lining goes back as far as you can go—all the way back to Africa. You want to remember someone and you always start off sad. But you don't want to cry about them being dead. You want to think about the good things they did. This makes everybody feel like they felt when he was alive."

Parasols twirled and handkerchiefs waved as the group paraded from the gravesite on Basin Street to Congo Square—now Louis "Satchmo" Armstrong Park—where slaves used to dance on Sunday.

Now was the time to face Dutch's death and move on. Julie, Cheri, and Monique had to return to other cities to mourn without family support—Julie to the Bay Area of California, Cheri to Denver, where she had recently taken a job, and Monique to Atlanta, where she was a sophomore at Emory University. I was concerned that the girls were not able to grieve at home. Both Julie and Cheri would have family friends nearby, but Monique had only her cadre of contemporaries. Before they all left, Janice Bodet, a friend and grief counselor, met with us and gave us comfort and counsel.

Dutch had lived a purposeful life, meeting challenges head on, rush-ing to overcome as many obstacles as he could, maybe sensing that his time was running out. His quest for social and racial justice fueled his achievements and sacrifices as he changed many lives for the good, brought people into the mainstream, and gave hope to his and future generations. His life was a model for making our country live up to its principles of justice and equality for all citizens. He had been the consummate teacher. As with his children, he made his points with his associates, especially the young, bright women and men with whom he worked. Every discussion was an opportunity to teach, to drive home a principle.

Thanks to generous contributions from friends and supporters, we established the Ernest N. Morial Memorial Foundation to continue Dutch's legacy. Several years later, the family would have an opportunity to triple the amount of the principal and dedicate it to the formation of the Ernest N. Morial Professorship in Public Policy and Public Affairs at Xavier University. Silas Lee continues as the first to hold the professorship. We remain grateful for the generosity of friends who made this possible with their initial contributions. Now, young college students learn to model leadership in helping to make a more just society.

When I finished writing the last thank-you notes to the many people who helped my family get through the tragedy, I realized I needed to get on with my life. What would that life be like? After thirty-four years of marriage to Dutch, facing all the challenges of our times together, I would be alone. Our children were being educated and doing well on their own. I had my challenging work at Xavier and several boards on which I was active. There would be no idle time, although Dutch's leaving would mean an empty place for all of us.

Dutch and I thought we would grow old together. But we were nowhere near that time in our lives. I believed we had more challenges to face together, although I did not know what they would be. Now that he was gone, I wondered, really, if he could have ever slowed down.

I thought about what the rest of my life alone would be like. I would miss the electricity Dutch generated whenever we talked about anything. I would miss his impatience to complete tasks. I would miss his waking in the middle of the night to jot down things he thought of lying awake, or maybe in his dreams.

⚜

Four years later, in 1993, New Orleans was abuzz with expectation of the upcoming race for mayor. The mayor's office was term limited, so the incumbent could not run. It was therefore an open race.

One afternoon, I was approached by several community leaders to be a candidate for mayor. The offer was somewhat unexpected—I was much involved in my job at Xavier—but I thought about it for several days. Finally, I told myself, *I can do this*. I knew New Orleans' challenges. I had lived here most of my life. I was politically active and had spent eight years as first lady watching Dutch's every crisis, every move he made to lead the city. I had an intimate knowledge of city government and how leadership shaped necessary changes.

The "Draft Sybil" momentum began to grow. I began to get excited about my own vision for the city and how I would go about putting a team together to construct that vision.

Up to that point, I had not had a serious conversation with my children about my running for mayor, but they were aware of others' interest in my candidacy. Marc was a Louisiana state senator at that time, and I knew I could count on his support. He also knew me and was wise enough to let the draft effort play out.

A loosely organized committee began talking up my candidacy in the community. It commissioned a poll to determine my viability before beginning to expand the draft effort. On a gray and rainy Sunday morning, Ed Renwick, who conducted the poll, called and reported that the race was mine to lose. My approval rating was above that of any other candidate listed in the poll.

The idea of running had carried me aloft for a while. But when I heard that the race was mine to lose, I came to my senses. I knew that this was not my destiny. Later, Marc told me he understood me well enough to know that I would not run. He was just thirty-five years old. I knew that he would likely consider his own potential candidacy at a later time.

The 1994 race for mayor began without me and without Marc. It wasn't until weeks later, when Marc saw the lineup of candidates, that he reconsidered—not my candidacy, but his own. He concluded that he could compete with any of the potential candidates, and this was his time. He had learned the ropes at the kitchen table. He and his brother, Jacques, had been involved in all of Dutch's campaigns. Marc knew the community and its needs. He knew what to do and when to do it. I was certain he would prove an enthusiastic candidate, and I became his most ardent supporter.

When Dutch first ran for mayor, he had already paid his dues. He had served as an attorney, civil rights attorney, community leader, assistant United States attorney, Louisiana state representative, juvenile-court judge, and appellate-court judge. He was a seasoned elected official. He was forty-eight years old when he was elected mayor of New Orleans.

Marc was just thirty-six when he took office. He had been a practicing attorney when his father passed away in 1989. Two years later, he won a seat in the Louisiana Senate, where he had a distinguished tenure. He established himself as a civil rights champion, serving as one of the plaintiffs to establish a seat of the Louisiana Supreme Court for an African American.

In 1993, when he decided to run for mayor, skeptics—even among friends—thought he was too young. But he ran a brilliant campaign, clearly addressing issues of public concern. By the time he took the oath of office, the skepticism about his inexperience had faded.

In fact, Marc represented a generational shift in city politics. He burst into the office of mayor with vigor and vision and proceeded to govern a city that had many problems. He assembled a team of young people, all of whom were ready to hit the ground running and were willing to work eighteen hours a day to accomplish their goals.

Marc and his team took a holistic approach and designed strategies to address interrelated problems. Public safety was a major challenge. Crime had escalated over the years to alarming rates, and citizens were gravely concerned. A plan to meet this challenge included selecting a new police superintendent and increasing police presence in neighborhoods. He also took action to curb police corruption and encouraged citizen participation in fighting crime. To reduce juvenile offenses, he instituted a curfew for young people under seventeen. Simultaneously, he established summer job opportunities and youth recreation programs including athletics and the arts to engage young people in healthy and productive activities. By the end of his first term, crime had been reduced dramatically.

Economic development was a major initiative during his administration. When plans to build a basketball arena near the Superdome were in jeopardy, he was instrumental in saving them and proved to be the driving force that brought professional basketball to New Orleans with the Hornets, now the Pelicans.

As his father had been, Marc was elected by his peer mayors of cities across the country to the presidency of the United States Conference of Mayors. At the end of his second term, New Orleans was a safer city. He left office with a 70 percent approval rating.

> *Oh Lord, give me more time,*
> *Been in the storm so long . . .*
>
> Negro spiritual

CHAPTER 23

Hell and High Water

When Dutch was judge in the juvenile court and I was teaching at Dunn School, we built our house on Harrison Avenue on the banks of Bayou St. John. In many ways, it was a harking back to the time shortly after our marriage when we lived with Dr. and Mrs. Thomas on an inlet of Chesapeake Bay. We had been so happy there—the memory of that time was so idyllic—that when we learned about the property for sale on the bayou in 1961, we immediately were attracted to it. We bought the undeveloped land and held it for twelve years before we could afford to build a house on it.

Bayou St. John, the only bayou located in New Orleans, had a fascinating history. In the early days, pirates trolled its waters. Before that, the Tangipahoa and other Native Americans used what they then called Bayou Choupic (Mudfish Bayou) for food, village sites, and transportation. The elegant houses that came to line the edges of the bayou over the centuries took the place of huts made from tree branches and palmetto leaves. Early peoples used the waterway to travel across Lake Pontchartrain and a footpath now known as Bayou Road to move overland to the Mississippi River for trading. Later, the French came hoping to establish themselves along the great river. A route from Lake Pontchartrain to Bayou Choupic led them to the Mississippi. New Orleans was established by the French on the crescent (upper ground) of the river. Now known as the French Quarter, this section is one of the highest parts of New Orleans. The nascent city was surrounded by a wall that was bounded by Rampart Street, Esplanade Avenue, Canal Street, and the Mississippi River. Bayou Choupic eventually became Bayou St. Jean and, later, Bayou St. John, but it was always used for exporting goods via the Mississippi. The destination was New Orleans, the end of the line for boats traveling down the Mississippi, a few of which Mark Twain piloted.

The home we built on Harrison Avenue was large enough to accommodate our five children. All the living areas and bedrooms faced the bayou, so we could see the water. I could watch the sunset from my room and from the solarium downstairs. Sometimes, the sunset over the bayou, the colors of the atmosphere, were so intense they would almost make me weep. Then the magical fifteen minutes would pass, and the sunset would be gone, the big yellow-orange ball descending behind the trees in City Park just beyond the bayou, leaving only the afterglow.

Mallard and Muscovy ducks, geese, herons, egrets, blue jays, cardinals, hummingbirds, purple martins, sparrows, sea gulls, starlings, and robins all shared the bayou with us. Brown pelicans, once an endangered species, visited occasionally. Squirrels feasted on the pecans that fell from the tree in our yard. Dutch had chosen the tree principally because it would attract those playful visitors. Year after year, they buried the nuts in the lawn and flower beds for the winter.

The only tree on the property when we purchased it was a redbud, which was covered in beautiful deep pink buds for a short time in the spring. Because it was in the footprint of the house, it fell to the bulldozer. But we planted more. In front of the house grew a Chinese pistachio, a Chinese elm, four hollies, and a beautifully shaped magnolia. In the back, we had a large peach tree from my father. He grew it from a seed from his own peach tree, and when it was a few feet high, he came over and planted it. Every spring, it had gorgeous pink blossoms, and then the peaches would weigh the tree down. Over the years, we added more trees, including a pear, a cypress, and three willows. One of my favorites was a large ash, a beautiful shade tree. Before it shed its leaves at the end of the year, it turned gold and rusty and glowed in the early-December light.

I have loved flowers all of my life, and I planted them everywhere. There were pink sasanquas and coral camellias; each bush must have produced at least fifty blossoms. They bloomed in December, around Christmas. The brilliant flowers were so dense you couldn't see the green leaves underneath. Pyracanthas grew wild and large in the subtropical climate, and these I spaced around the pool fence. I would cut the branches in the fall to bring inside to make Thanksgiving and Christmas arrangements, risking my hands because the stems had thorns. In a little Japanese garden right behind the dining room, the dwarf junipers and gardenias surrounded a stone Japanese lantern.

The yard and the adjacent bayou gave our children an understanding of the natural world that they might not have gotten in other places in the city. One spring, a goose laid eleven eggs in the Japanese garden. At mealtimes, we could look out the window—which went down to the baseboard—and observe. Her guard was a ferocious male who honked and stretched his neck at us if we came near. She sat and sat and then one day abandoned the nest. We were never able to figure out why—maybe she knew it was not safe. That very day, crows swooped down, cracked open the eggs, and feasted on them. It was a hard thing to watch—not pretty but instructive.

One summer morning, I heard Monique, who was about five, screaming at the top of her lungs, "Mommy, help, help, help!" I rushed out, my heart pounding, to see her perched on top of the picnic table, two geese nearly as big as herself honking furiously at her. I chased them with a broom and held her in my arms. "They were after me," she cried. "They were after me!"

As they got older, the children made the house on the bayou their own. When Marc was a teenager, he took care of the lawn, mowing the grass on the riding mower. He took pride in his work; I found him many times smiling in admiration when he was finished. From her room, Cheri often sketched lovely views of the bayou, recording the flora and fauna of the season. Julie, too, found solace in the garden, expressing a keen interest in whatever was blooming each season. Jacques took to fishing off the pier, a skill he learned on trips with my father. Once, he went swimming in the bayou, only to discover why no one ever tried. The water was brackish and the bottom muddy, though it fed the wildlife for miles around.

Dutch and I had lived on Bayou St. John for sixteen years when he died. All of the children were gone by then. Monique was still in college in Atlanta. It never occurred to me to move. I had memories to savor and loved the house, the yard, the bayou. Two years later, Monique was back with me to attend Tulane Law School.

Looking across the bayou, Dutch and I often watched rainstorms coming into New Orleans. In the early hours of the day, the great dark clouds loomed over the horizon and lightning flashed across the water. Sometimes, the bayou water was still and looked like a sheet of glass. Over the years, there were many storms, but no major hurricanes struck New Orleans. Even Hurricane Camille, as destructive as it was for the lower Louisiana Gulf Coast in 1969, had spared New Orleans and much of Louisiana.

Hurricanes, though, especially major ones, were always a threat. The

Monique, Julie, Dutch, Marc, Sybil, Cheri, and Jacques in the backyard at
Bayou St. John
<small>AUTHOR'S COLLECTION</small>

city is below sea level and is protected by levees. Its topography is much
like that of the traditional gumbo bowl, with a flat upper edge around a
concave hollow. The bowl made for some interesting experiences. For
instance, you could sit in a café next to the levee and watch boats passing above you. As the city's population grew, approaching five hundred
thousand by the year 2000, many more residents came to live on the
lower ground, the "bowl" of New Orleans.

On August 23, 2005, I was driving home from the pharmacy when
I heard the weather report on the car radio: tropical storm Katrina was
building up strength as it entered the warm waters of the Gulf of Mexico.

Ten tropical storms had formed already that year. While Florida was particularly hard hit, so far Louisiana had been spared. The meteorolo-gists' long list of names had traveled down to the letter K. Katrina sound-ed like a pretty name. It didn't sound like a hurricane. I did not consider that Louisiana's good luck might run out—not in the dead of August, not this year, not now.

The storm had formed in the skies over the Bahamas. It crossed southern Florida on August 25 but was then a comparatively weak Cat-egory 1 hurricane that had caused a few deaths and flooding. But now, Katrina was strengthening in the warm waters of the gulf. Initially, it ap-peared that the storm would turn north and come ashore on the already battered Florida Panhandle. The Louisiana coast was only one of several destinations where Katrina might strike.

As teenagers, Jean and I had reeled through a pair of hurricanes at sea. As a young mother, I had experienced the mayhem of Hurricane Betsy crashing through my parents' doors and flooding our home. If the respite since then—four decades without a hurricane—had mesmerized me somewhat, I still knew what hurricanes could do.

Wherever the storm was going, I needed to make sure I was ready. I checked my hurricane supplies: batteries for the radio and flashlights, water, and nonperishable foods. I needed a non-electric can opener. I thought I'd better go to the store before the shops got crowded and sup-plies disappeared.

New Orleans relies on its levees to hold back the moat of water around it—the Mississippi River and Lake Pontchartrain. And much like a ship, it relies on a system of pumps to get rid of the water when it does not drain fast enough. During the forty years since Hurricane Betsy, the Army Corps of Engineers had done work on the levees. The general consensus was that they would probably hold against a moderate hur-ricane. Now, as Katrina moved west into the summer-heated waters of the gulf, it was becoming something other than moderate. In fact, it soon doubled in size and increased significantly in strength. At the same time, it took a more westerly path. If it did hit New Orleans, depending on exactly where it struck and the time of day, the levees might hold against the storm surge and tides. By Sunday, August 28, though, Katrina was a huge Category 4 storm. As the monster hurricane took aim at the central Gulf Coast, Mayor Ray Nagin ordered the city to evacuate.

I had hoped to leave on Saturday afternoon, before mandatory evacuation, but my plans changed because of the death and funeral of a dear friend, Clarence Barney, who had led the New Orleans Urban League for thirty years. The funeral was to be held at the Dillard University chapel, and Marc, as president and CEO of the National Urban League, was slated to give the eulogy. After the service, he planned to leave for the airport in Baton Rouge for his return flight to New York, as the New Orleans airport was closed. By then, though, the voluntary exodus from the city had clogged the highway. Marc knew he could not get to Baton Rouge in time for his flight, and there were no other flights until six the next morning. I postponed my evacuation, and Marc spent the night with me at the Harrison Avenue house. He left for the airport before dawn on Sunday.

Shortly afterward, I picked up Julie's children—Martine, seven, and Mathieu, three. Julie and her husband, Juan, would travel to Cheri's home in Baton Rouge after me. We headed out of the city on Interstate 10. By then, the exodus was escalating. The bumper-to-bumper traffic moved at five to ten miles per hour at best. The drive, which normally was an hour and a half, took us four hours.

"When are we going to get there, Grammy?"

I had heard that question from the backseat about a half-dozen times by then. Each time, I tried to sound optimistic. "We're more than halfway there," I said several times.

Cheri had lived in Baton Rouge for five years with her husband, Verge. They had two boys, Austin, who was two, and Jaiden, just months old. We weren't the only ones evacuating to Cheri's house. Most of our immediate family—seven adults and a dog, to be exact—would soon converge on her location. Monique was already on her way. Juan followed after moving the rugs and art to the second floor of his and Julie's home. She would not arrive until Monday; Jacques would follow after her.

Cheri and Verge were welcoming and hospitable to all of us in a situation that was anything but comforting. Their neighbors brought food, sheets, and towels as everyone settled in. Verge's parents, the Ausberrys, came from New Iberia in their car, which was loaded with enough food—some of it cooked—to feed an army. They even offered a credit card to purchase anything we needed, including clothes, since we had only one or two changes.

For most of the first day, we were glued to the television, watching as the hurricane, which now stretched across the entire Gulf of Mexico, powered toward us. At one point on Sunday, it was measured at a Category 5, indicating its potential to inflict the worst devastation possible. Against that kind of force, no New Orleans levee, and virtually no house in the city, would stand.

Early Monday morning, Katrina, by then diminished to Category 4, made three successive landfalls along the Gulf Coast. The third, with the hurricane at Category 3 strength, was not exactly at New Orleans, but slightly east. The 120-miles-per-hour winds piled up the waters of huge Lake Pontchartrain and dumped them into Slidell and other bordering areas. Those residents whose houses were still standing noticed their yards were filled with dead fish.

We waited to learn how New Orleans would hold against the storm surge. When Katrina hit New Orleans, it was raining in Baton Rouge. The gale-force winds and heavy rain did not come around to us until the second day, Tuesday, as the broad cloud bands moved counterclockwise, across and up the Mississippi River.

Those same winds drove the waters of the river along the levees in New Orleans. Early Monday morning, there were reports of water going over and through the city's levees. By late Monday morning, as Julie arrived in Baton Rouge, the 17th Street Canal, at the west end of the city, had been breached. One after another, reports came in of embankments giving way. The London Avenue Canal breached, flooding the Gentilly area, where I lived. The floodwaters did not come from the bayou at the back of the house, but from the front, Harrison Avenue. The flooded neighborhoods were announced each in their turn on the television, which carried hurricane news all day. By Tuesday, 80 percent of New Orleans was underwater.

My house, as well as Julie's and Monique's, which were near mine, flooded. The roof of Jacques's house collapsed, the water rushing in from above. We faced despair as we realized that, among us, we had no home fit to live in. With the exception of Cheri in Baton Rouge and Marc in New York, we were, all of us, homeless.

Our stories were but a small part of the huge nightmare unfolding for all of New Orleans. Our faces were glued to the television and the continuous news of the seemingly unstoppable devastation. Roughly a hundred thousand people were stranded in the flooded city. We looked in horror at the people who could not leave because they had no means of getting anywhere and, often as not, because they had nowhere to go. Most were eventually taken, usually by bus, to the two shelters, the Superdome and the Ernest N. Morial Convention Center. When no bus was available, some people walked miles from their homes to those shelters.

The sites were not prepared with provisions. Evacuees had only a roof overhead as protection from the pounding rain and wind. Without electricity, there was no air conditioning, so the sweltering heat and humidity inside the windowless buildings was suffocating. Initially, those people had no water, no food, no medical presence. After a few days of overuse of the lavatories, the plumbing failed. These facilities were supposed to be shelters for survivors, but before it was over, some died. And

Hurricane Katrina looms over the Gulf of Mexico, waiting to strike.
NOAA

then there were people who did not get into the shelters, some of whom drowned or died in the heat, waiting sometimes days for help that did not arrive in time.

People and organizations were trying to help, but it was difficult, if not impossible. A colleague with whom I served on a board brought cases of water to the convention center and was told he couldn't enter. He said, "I don't need to come in. Just take them and pass them around to the people." But the guards refused to take the bottles. I could not help thinking in absolute horror about the condition of the people inside, knowing how Dutch would have felt if he knew people would be treated that way in a building that was named for him.

The city seemed both helpless and hopeless. Viewing the situation from Baton Rouge, that's also the way we felt—helpless and hopeless to do anything. We had little respite from the wrenching frustration, especially at night. Sleep was sporadic; often, I was startled awake by the sound of the wind or a disturbing dream.

During the day, we tried to keep our spirits up so the children wouldn't become fearful. The menagerie at Cheri and Verge's house—they and their two boys and all seven of us refugees—bonded in a way we never could have planned. We sat around after dinner trying to talk about anything other than the hurricane. The atmosphere was tense at times, because we were all anxious about our futures. We tried not to spend all of our time watching the nightmare unfold on television, but we had to know what was happening.

As the crisis seemed only to get worse, watching those images was frustrating; there seemed to be such a lack of response to the titanic disaster. I could not help thinking, as many did, *Is this America?* My husband and my son had been mayors of New Orleans, and I knew there was a disaster plan for the city. They had talked about it. Why wasn't it being implemented? We had all seen the tremendous national mobilization in the wake of 9/11. Why weren't the rescue resources of our great country in evidence here, now? The languishing people in New Orleans were less like victims of a natural disaster and more like victims of war, begging for water, begging for help, pleading for their sick and dying family members. At times, I could no longer watch the television screen. We agreed to turn it off for a while, so we could get some moments of relief from the trauma.

Six days after the levees broke and New Orleans flooded, my cousin Madonna's daughter, Madonna-Ann, rang Cheri's doorbell urgently, then rushed into the house in tears. Her husband followed close behind. Without introduction, she wailed, "I can't find my mother. She isn't answering her cell phone, and I can't reach any of her friends. Mama has my daughter with her. I am worried they didn't get out of the city before the floodwaters came in."

We could give her no solace; we had not heard from Madonna. But we told her we would call everyone we could to try to find her, and would let her know immediately when we had any news. She and her husband went back to LaPlace (the town where they had fled from the flood), some thirty miles from New Orleans. She said she would call us every day for any news.

Reaching anyone who had fled the city was virtually impossible. Without electricity, cell phones could not be charged. Many had left their homes and had no way to contact family and loved ones. Madonna-Ann's plight was sad but familiar.

What we didn't know, and would find out only days later, was what had happened to Madonna during Katrina. Before the hurricane, she evacuated with her own elderly mother, her nine-year-old daughter, her granddaughter (Madonna-Ann's daughter), and her brother to the Hyatt Hotel, a seemingly safe place in the Central Business District, next to the Superdome. Although the area was on the "ridge" of the city and was not flooded, the Hyatt's windows blew out from the force of the 120-mile-per-hour hurricane winds. The evacuees at the hotel were forced to leave. Night was near, and New Orleans was without electricity—no street-lights. Madonna's car was parked in a garage between the Hyatt and the Superdome, so she and her family walked over to the Superdome, look-ing for shelter.

When she saw the conditions there—crowds of frantic people and no food or water—she turned away. She and her family went back to her car in the parking garage and spent the night there. They were not alone; other people were also in the dark parking garage, taking shelter in their cars.

When dawn broke, Madonna got out of the car to assess the situ-ation. She saw that buses were picking up people. She and her family abandoned the car and ran to the staging area. She spoke to someone in charge and managed to get her family on a bus. They had no idea where they were going at that point, but they were together.

After several hours, the bus stopped at a shelter in Alexandria, Loui-siana, about 220 miles from New Orleans. But Madonna and her family and the other passengers were turned away because the shelter was full to capacity. The bus continued to the next town, Pineville, where Madonna knew no one. The family spent several days there in a designated shelter until being assigned to a trailer. Eventually, Madonna was able to reach her family, including Madonna-Ann. They were reunited, but it had been a horrific experience for the entire family.

Just after the hurricane passed, aircraft sponsored by the National Oceanic and Atmospheric Administration took over seven thousand images of flooded New Orleans. Those images were assembled into a montage. Eventually, visitors to a website could click on any neighborhood that had been affected by the flooding. Two weeks after Hurricane Katrina, Jacques pulled up an aerial view of my underwater neighborhood. I gasped as I looked at the bayou in my backyard and on Harrison Avenue, which were now all one. It turned out that bayou flooding was not to blame, but rather the overflowing of the London Avenue Canal about a mile away.

⚜

Three weeks later, when the waters had receded and I could get to my house on two feet, rather than in a boat, I arranged to meet with the insurance adjuster. He would assess my damages, and I would then have some idea of my recovery potential.

I arrived at my house on Bayou St. John simultaneously with the adjuster. He got out of his car, eager to start what was at this point a routine for him. I hadn't even had a chance to look at my flooded house or what was left of the property. I looked at him, wanting to be polite but knowing I could not begin just yet.

"Give me a minute, please. I need a minute."

I made an effort to compose myself. I didn't want to appear weak, not in front of a stranger. I could see the damage to the outside of the house—debris strewn everywhere, muddy residue blanketing the place—but that was secondary. In many ways, it was the land and trees outside that brought grief to my eyes. Over the years, this landscape had brought so much joy to me. The great trees I had nurtured lay in muddy heaps. There were no flowers. The small pier on the bayou was crushed. I turned and noticed the remains of the picnic table where Monique had taken refuge from the geese that spring morning long ago. All the beautiful birds had fled. Their homeplace, their refuge, was gone. As was mine.

The water, eight inches of it, had pushed through the lower level of my house. The furniture had floated in the flood. Instead of flowing out, as it had in our home on Press Drive during Hurricane Betsy, the water remained in the house for three weeks. The heat and humidity drove black mold up the walls, and a gray fuzz settled on each piece of furniture. Much of what I'd collected and begun to archive of our family history—photographs, films, mementos, letters—was destroyed.

Thanks to Jacques and Monique, I was spared the worst of it. As soon as the water receded, they had armed themselves with tetanus and hepatitis shots. Wearing boots, long pants, long-sleeved shirts, gloves, hats, and masks, they had ventured into my house to try to stop the mold that was consuming everything on the first floor. They waded through the ankle-deep water on the street and sidewalk to enter. They threw out the rugs and carpets, emptied the spoiled food from the refrigerator, and scraped the muck that had settled on the floors. Then they mopped down the entire first floor with bleach and disinfectant. Finally, they gathered a few things that were not soaked or moldy. I am forever grateful to them for relieving me of the first sight of the destruction.

The insurance adjuster finally completed his task. As I left my home, driving through the devastated neighborhoods, I began to think about my friends and other New Orleans people who had lived in areas that flooded to the rooftops, who had lost everything, as Monique had. (Her house was so badly damaged that it had to be demolished.) Some people had nowhere to evacuate and were transported to places unknown, as Madonna was, their lives completely broken apart. I thought about the Lower Ninth Ward, a community completely destroyed, once filled with working and retired people who were homeowners, some living on pensions, others eking out a living, good, solid citizens who might never recover. Dutch and I had lived in that district, in the Upper Ninth Ward, as young married people. Now, the Lower Ninth was all but abandoned in the aftermath of not just one disaster, but two: a hurricane, then national neglect. How would those people get their lives back? How would they raise their children? What would they retire to?

⚜

Ten days after Katrina, Jacques and Monique left Cheri's house to return to New Orleans. They stayed temporarily with friends who were spared the flooding. Now, they each had to figure out their work situation. It would take years before both of them were back on their feet. I was still in Baton Rouge, as were Julie and her family. She had registered her children in the Baton Rouge schools while she commuted to Tulane University Medical Center in New Orleans. She worked there as a physician for a short time, while the medical facilities in the city were crashing. A short time later, she got a position in Baton Rouge, and she and her family moved into an apartment there.

After two months, realizing I needed somewhere semi-permanent to live, I moved into an apartment in Baton Rouge. None of us had any clear picture of our immediate future, nor could we really plan at this time. We had to live in the moment.

After hours, and sometimes days, of searching, I finally knew where my extended family and friends were. Within a year, my friend Lydia Adams, who had evacuated to Chattanooga, Tennessee, where her son and his family lived, had tracked (thanks to cell phones) many of our friends flung everywhere from east to west in this country. Many had lost their homes, but they were alive and safe. It was a miracle, really, because so many were left so terribly *unsafe*. A thousand had drowned in the waters that engulfed the city.

What happened in New Orleans was a natural catastrophe, but it was also a national disgrace. To talk about New Orleans being on its knees after Katrina was a vast understatement. The city, like many urban areas, had been on its knees for years, cut off from federal programs and initiatives that were voted down one after another. When the War on Poverty programs ended after the Johnson administration, there was little to replace them. Decades of neglect had erased the sense that most of the residents mattered to anyone. Katrina merely revealed what already existed. Aside from its tourism, offshore oil, and port trade, New Orleans wasn't of consequence to the nation at large. Its people had been abandoned long before the hurricane swept its degraded levees and other protections away. As the floodwaters receded, the city wasn't on its knees, but lying face down in the mud.

Some looked at the disaster and felt a strange sense of vindication. It was obvious to them that such a population—many of whom were poor—was incapable of saving itself, of evacuating properly, of harnessing its energies and digging out of disaster. But this was a blithely narrow observation. New Orleans collapsed and stayed collapsed not only because of the severity of the devastation—although that was significant—but also because of the decades of dissolution and federal neglect of the nation's urban economies, structures, and programs.

After the *Brown* decision striking down segregated schools, the flight of the white middle class to the suburbs had eroded New Orleans' tax base. Diminishing resources for schools contributed to the erosion of the quality of education. These conditions were not restricted to New Orleans. Many of the country's urban areas were affected by the dismantling of the War on Poverty programs, which provided opportunities for job training, small-business incentives and assistance, and other initiatives that could lift the poor and disadvantaged to levels of independence. The abandonment of these programs left the underclass, the forgotten, trapped. As Marc astutely put it, "Katrina put it out there. No one can play the pretend game anymore that there isn't poverty and inequality in this country."

It should come as a surprise to no thinking person that sporadic intervention does little to alleviate entrenched social ills. If the problems of education, nutrition, and housing are going to be alleviated, they have to be addressed consistently. There has to be reliable, year-after-year remediation of the decades of neglect to assist people needing help to become productive citizens. My personal belief, after years of working in the field, is that the solution begins with a quality education for all. It does not guarantee an even playing field, but it makes one more possible.

While there was compassion and concern among many throughout the country, the oil pipelines were replaced and repaired much more expeditiously than the levees. Today, much of New Orleans' Ninth Ward still looks like a disaster area. Now, tourists come to that New Orleans to see the devastation. But human beings lived there; many owned homes and tried to raise their children with dignity, as Dutch and I had in the 1960s. Those families were abandoned after Katrina.

Looking at the stricken neighborhoods, I could not help remembering the beautiful city I had grown up in. I recalled North Claiborne Avenue with its crowds of shoppers and canopies of oak trees. In my little neighborhood on Miro Street, mixed races and economic classes had managed to live in peace. When the Civil Rights Movement began, all of that changed. North Claiborne disappeared; it was uprooted and destroyed. Was it our desire to be treated just as any other human beings that destroyed the city? Who had abandoned it? Where had it gone? What did that loss say about the United States of America?

Whatever condemnation needs to be made, it should not be applied universally. Aid did come from good people, who tried to help in large and small ways. While New Orleans lacked the political clout necessary to lift the city out of the morass after Katrina, it did have friends, good friends, from around the globe. In the period following the storm, and continuing to this day, they rose up and said, as President Johnson had while visiting the Ninth Ward during Hurricane Betsy, "I am here to help you."

Thousands of individuals and groups—including church groups, diverse organizations, and college students from all over the country and the world—came to New Orleans to lend their time and hands. Some have made the journey successive times, at much personal cost, to help restore our city. Many from nearby and far-off places have opened their wallets over and over. In word and in deed, they have asserted that New Orleans is an inimitable city and deserves to be saved. It is this generosity of care and giving that has renewed my faith in the goodness of humanity.

After Katrina, New Orleans' population dropped by more than half, to just over 230,000. Ten years later, many New Orleans residents still have not returned to their city. There are many reasons. After so many demolitions—over seven hundred—fewer houses are left for them. Many neighborhoods are still abandoned, as mine is; many people have little means or capacity to recover. Their jobs are often gone, and there is little housing for what workers are needed. The city has lost much of the African American middle class who lived in the Gentilly and New Orleans East neighborhoods, which were destroyed by the flooding of the London Avenue Canal. Many churches, the bedrock of neighborhoods and extended families, were destroyed or damaged beyond use. The public-school system was crippled. Recovery has proven an uphill struggle. The injury, the wounding of New Orleans, has been deep and slow to heal.

Yet New Orleans is a city familiar with catastrophe. Although it is called "the Big Easy," it has not had an easy history. Over the centuries, it has faced challenges that few cities in America have known. In the middle of the nineteenth century, the city suffered one of the first civilian bombardments in the Civil War. It has also withstood the nation's worst epidemics. Cholera struck New Orleans in 1832 and took over four thousand lives; nearly eight thousand were lost to yellow fever in 1853. Yellow fever continued to wreak havoc upon the city's population into the twentieth century.

Nevertheless, New Orleans recovered from all these disasters and grew. Now, the city is slowly but surely recovering. Finally, a state-of-the-art levee system is being put in place so that New Orleans residents need no longer live in perpetual fear of another Katrina. Increasing numbers are making the journey back and restoring their homes; small businesses, the heart of New Orleans, are recovering. The return of previous residents, as well as new arrivals, have bolstered the city's population, now closing in on four hundred thousand. Most importantly, the spirit of the people of New Orleans, the unique culture of this Crescent City, is rebounding and nourishing the recovery.

*How long? Not long. How long? Not long,
because the arc of the moral universe is long,
but it bends toward justice.*

Martin Luther King Jr.

CHAPTER 24

A President Who Looks Like Us

My granddaughter Martine and I jumped out of the taxi and into the freezing New Jersey air; we were just outside Newark's Liberty Train Station and anxious to get inside, out of the cold. Martine had accompanied me on the flight from Baton Rouge. Soon, my daughter-in-law Michelle and her children, Mason, seven, and Margeaux, three, would arrive with their nanny, Hope. Huddled in our warm coats, we gathered in the main hall of the station. We were excited as we waited to get on the train to Washington, but there was a delay.

Mason, who had traveled several times to Washington with his father, Marc, kept watching the big board that announced arrivals and departures. "There it is!" he exclaimed around six-thirty when the track was announced. "It's late! It's late!"

Just then, a redcap appeared with a luggage cart and told us that President-elect Barack Obama was responsible for the delay. He had chosen to travel by special train that afternoon from Philadelphia to Washington, just as a previous Illinois president, Abraham Lincoln, had done almost 150 years before.

The inauguration of any president is exciting, but Barack Obama's was uniquely inspiring for us because he, his wife, and daughters were African Americans. I had seen some astonishing things in my life, but I did not think I would live to see a person of my own race at the helm of our government.

Still, I knew a little about life as "the first," since Dutch had so often played that role, especially as the first black to serve as mayor of New Orleans. After Dutch's death in 1989, Marc had served as mayor from 1994 to 2002.

I knew about being married to an elected official, and I also knew about the challenge of rearing a family in the limelight, sometimes under threats that chilled me to the marrow. I suspected that the Obamas were learning about this, and I prayed for their safety. I also prayed that their daughters would come through it as well as my own children had.

Martine was spellbound. She had been enamored with Barack Obama before anyone else thought he had a chance to receive the Democratic nomination. She listened to news of the campaign on public radio as her mother, Julie, drove her and her brother, Mathieu, to school. Then she read everything she could find about Obama in newspapers and magazines. She celebrated when he was nominated and finished her homework early to watch the presidential debates. Of course, she cheered loudest when he was elected. Hers was the kind of buoyant excitement Obama stirred among young adults, teens, and children.

Personally, I had been impressed with Obama's poise and sincerity when he delivered the keynote address at the 2004 Democratic National Convention. When he announced his candidacy for president, I decided he was "my" candidate. But experience (and history) had taught me that there were many obstacles to the candidacy of any African American. When the exposé of his minister's sermons was aired over and over on

television, my heart sank. Then, when he gave a speech in response—
"A More Perfect Union," addressing race in America—I knew he had a
chance. Would this open the dialogue on race that had been repressed
for so long? Or would race be the determining factor in his defeat? He
drew the title of his address from the Preamble to the Constitution. Back
in the early 1960s when the Louisiana League of Good Government
was preparing black citizens to register to vote, one of the requirements
was a literacy test. And what were they asked to read? The Preamble. My
thoughts went back to those eager people who wanted to have a voice
and were petrified just thinking of the process they had to endure. I could
hear them now: "We the People of the United States, in Order to form a
more perfect Union . . ." They read it over and over, nearly committing it
to memory, because they wanted to vote.

I am not a person prone to weeping. As a public figure, I have had to
restrain my emotions on many occasions. On November 4, 2008, though,
when Barack Obama's election became a reality, my tears would not stop.
They were tears of joy, tears of relief, tears of pride in my country that
a majority of its people chose a brilliant, charismatic young American
despite his race.

Stony indeed had been the road trod by African Americans from
slavery through Jim Crow, from the Civil Rights Movement to political
empowerment. Now, a black man born in 1961 would hold the highest
office in the land. Could it have been fifty-five years since that summer
when I met Dutch and we talked excitedly about the just-delivered Supreme Court ruling in *Brown v. Board of Education*? Yes, it had.

By the time we arrived at Union Station in Washington, it was 11:45 P.M.
Just as we stepped off the train, Mason shouted, "There it is! There's Barack
Obama's coach! It is green and black and looks like a bullet!" We had to
hustle him away so we could exit the station.

Marc was waiting with help to take our luggage. I could feel the excitement in the air as the crowd moved to the exit, all in good spirits and
easy conversation. Outside our hotel, people were in the frigid air, not

moving nearly as quickly as my Southern blood would have dictated. We bustled into the lobby, filled with happy people, and went to our rooms to rest up for what would come next.

Sunday was no warmer. After breakfast in Marc and Michelle's suite, we bundled up again and took the children to the National Mall. After visiting two exhibits at the National Air and Space Museum, we walked out onto the mall itself. A bitter wind was blowing, and we looked up to the Capitol, where the inauguration would take place. Then we turned around to see the Washington Monument and, in the distance, the Lincoln Memorial. Close to two million people would crowd into this space for the swearing-in.

Marc has been president of the National Urban League since 2003. Our last event Sunday was the league's reception at the Museum for Women in the Arts. Martine, Mason, and Margeaux all attended, the girls beautiful in their party dresses and Mason handsome in his suit and tie. Everyone—black, white, Latino, Asian, African, and Middle Eastern— was euphoric as Marc, in his remarks, recognized the sacrifices that had brought us to this moment.

Although Coretta Scott King had died in 2006, her spirit and that of her husband, Martin, was everywhere that weekend. Monday was Dr. Martin Luther King Day, the celebration of his birthday, and Marc had been asked to introduce the speaker at a breakfast hosted by the United States Conference of Mayors, an organization he and his father had both led. Mayors from all over the country—Democratic and Republican—gathered to hear former president Bill Clinton.

In his remarks, Marc told the audience, "Two years ago, Martine, my niece who is nine, whispered in my ear, 'Uncle Marc, I am going to be president of the United States when I grow up.' "

That got a lot of applause, and Martine, who was there with me, Mason, and Marc's wife, Michelle, whispered, "I can't believe he told everybody!"

Later, we went backstage and had our photo taken with former president Clinton. As she shook his hand, Martine said, "I have a friendship bracelet just like yours that I made."

"I'll tell you where I got it," President Clinton said. "I was on a mission overseas, and some children gave it to me to thank me. I'm sure they made it just like you did."

She was thrilled that he had spoken to her. Then it was on to lunch.

Earl W. Stafford, a wealthy African American, knew what a momentous event the election was to millions of our people. Through his Stafford Foundation, he arranged and funded travel and lodging for several hundred low-income African Americans to come to Washington. They were in attendance at the luncheon, held in a big downtown hotel. It began with the singing of "Lift Every Voice and Sing," James Weldon Johnson's rousing song, often called "the Negro National Anthem." It was followed by recitations and tributes by children and teens and a keynote speech by Martin Luther King III, son of the slain civil rights leader. Mason, Martine, and the other children present seemed captivated by the ceremony.

Later in the day, the children attended a concert for the young set at one of the Smithsonian museums while Michelle and I attended the "Let Freedom Swing" concert at the Kennedy Center. It was presented by New Orleans native Wynton Marsalis, who had graciously performed at Dutch's funeral and whom we knew well. He is now artistic director of jazz at Lincoln Center in New York. We left the concert and raced in the cold to a reception at the Newseum sponsored by the *Huffington Post*, but it was so crowded that we decided to return to our hotel. Once there, we quickly discovered that Bruce Springsteen, who had performed at the Lincoln Memorial in another concert, was on hand, so we met him, too.

All this, I marveled later, happened before the big day.

Upon waking on Tuesday, January 20, I looked out the window of my room. In the bitter cold, people were moving in droves in what looked like a pilgrimage—fifteen and twenty across, making their way to the National Mall for the inauguration. They were all wrapped up, only their eyes visible, because they would be standing in the weather for four hours before the event began. It was nineteen degrees on Inauguration Day—not an unusual temperature at this latitude, but cold beyond comprehension for a Louisiana resident.

The historic event was scheduled for noon. Marc had reserved a hotel room with a huge television screen for friends who were not up to braving the frigid weather. Along with many veterans of the Civil Rights Movement, I planned to watch from there.

Marc had three reserved tickets for the actual ceremony. He said to Mason, "It is really freezing outside, and we will be out in the cold for two or three hours. You can stay here where it is warm and see it all on the big screen."

To which Mason replied, "I didn't take off from school to watch Barack Obama get sworn in on television. I want to go with you and Mommy."

How could I not recall the times his father had insisted upon accompanying Dutch?

Hope was taking Martine and Margeaux to a spot farther back on the mall, but by the time they arrived, the gate was closed, so they returned to the hotel's warmth as well. With one eye on the huge screen, where the cameras panned across the sea of people, we veterans shared stories, talking about the long struggle that had paved the way for this milestone. I was sure millions of families and friends all over the country—nay, the world—were engaged as we were, although we were only a stone's throw from the event and could feel the electric atmosphere. One veteran exclaimed, "This is a halleluiah day!"

As the Obama family stepped to the podium, the crowd hushed and the mood became reverent. Malia and Sasha, the Obama children, stood by as their mother, Michelle, held the very Bible on which Abraham Lincoln had placed his hand when he was sworn in as president. As Barack Obama placed his hand upon that book, tears flowed unashamedly from both men and women within our enclave.

Then, while the whole world watched, President Obama delivered his sober and solemn Inaugural Address. His words offered his vision for America and the changes he believed would restore our stature at home and abroad. He spoke about the progress the inauguration represented:

> This is the meaning of our liberty and our creed, why men and women and children of every race and every faith can join in celebration across this magnificent mall; and why a man whose father less than sixty years ago might not have been served in a local restaurant can now stand before you to take a most sacred oath. . . .
>
> Let it be said by our children's children that when we were tested we refused to let this journey end, that we did not turn back nor did we falter, and with eyes fixed on the horizon and God's grace upon us, we carried forth that great gift of freedom and delivered it safely to future generations.

Marc, Michelle, and Mason returned from the National Mall frozen but thrilled at having witnessed this event. All afternoon, everyone was in a festive mood, and the inaugural balls beckoned.

I had been to the White House with Dutch during the Johnson administration and again during the Carter years. I had also attended Bill Clinton's inaugural ball. This time, I'd be attending two!

With Hope's assistance, Martine, Mason, and Margeaux were busy dressing in their party clothes and bundling up for the Children's Ball. Meanwhile, Marc, Michelle, and I dressed to attend the Obama Home States Ball, sponsored by Hawaii and Illinois. This was the ball attended by Oprah Winfrey, T. D. Jakes, and many Obama intimates. Other guests came from all over the country. Everyone, dressed in formal finery, was euphoric. The first lady and the president walked hand in hand onto the stage to thunderous cheering; he greeted us and thanked us for sharing the day with him and his family. Then he and Michelle danced to Beyoncé's "At Last" before they left to attend other balls.

We left, too, to attend the Civil Rights Presidential Inaugural Gala and to meet up with my granddaughter Kemah, Marc's oldest child, who was in graduate school in Washington. That meant traveling through the icy cold from the convention center to the hotel where the gala was to be held. Upon arrival, we entered another warm and invigorating event, where we met more old friends as the band played. Many danced.

My energy was winding down, and I wanted to savor the long and wonderful day. We climbed into the car and returned to the hotel, where the lobby was full of people. Since Martine was spending the night with her cousins Mason and Margeaux, I had the room to myself. It was two in the morning, and we still had to pack. Rather than fall into a deep sleep that would be short lived, I dreamily reviewed the events of the inauguration, savored its significance, and remembered the long history that had brought us here. Before I knew it, it was five o'clock and time to get up and go to the train station.

⚜

A little more than two years later, under a deep summer sky, I got an even more personal view of the Obama presidency during the National Urban League's centennial celebration in Washington.

Coast Guard admiral Stephen Rochon, director of the residence and chief usher of the White House, is from New Orleans. He had been captain of the port of New Orleans during Marc's tenure as mayor. He agreed to take us on a private tour of the White House. When he met us in a reception room there, he greeted us with a surprise: "The timing of your arrival is serendipitous. President Obama will be boarding Marine One, the presidential helicopter, shortly. Would you like to see him board?" My grandchildren were thrilled. He said, "Come on out to the South Lawn and wait. It should be only a few minutes."

The day was one of the hottest that year, the sun blazing down as we waited for what we thought would be just a few minutes. But the president was delayed, so the wait was longer. The sun overhead was fiery and unmitigated by the slightest cloud cover. I was holding on to Jacques's arm when, before I knew what was happening, I fainted, right there on the South Lawn of the White House.

My daughter Julie, who is a doctor and was steps away, came immediately to attend to me. She was interrupted, however, when out of the blue two White House physicians appeared with oxygen. By then, I had revived somewhat and was staring into the faces of my children and grandchildren. They had been diverted from the real drama about to happen and were now staring at me with concerned expressions. The medical staff of the White House took me into the Oval Reception Room, where the president received dignitaries arriving by helicopter. After checking my vitals, questioning me, and giving me some water, they determined that the heat had just gotten to me.

I was placed in a wheelchair and rolled out to rejoin my family. It was a good thing the president was late, for my drama and his might have coincided. I was a bit embarrassed, even though my family members were the only ones present. I felt physically fine. Later, though, I discovered my ankle was badly injured.

When the helicopter landed on the South Lawn, we were standing a safe but relatively close distance away. Now, of course, came the real excitement for my grandchildren. As the rotors beat up a wind, seven-year-old Mathieu exclaimed, "It's like a hurricane!" He had experienced both Katrina and Rita in 2005.

Shortly afterward, President Obama came out of the West Wing, walked across the lawn, and waved to us as the children gleefully waved back. Before he boarded, he turned around and waved one more time. We then followed Admiral Rochon on the tour.

President Barack Obama, Sybil, and her son Marc Morial
AUTHOR'S COLLECTION

Later, during the Urban League's conference, Michelle, Kemah, Mason, Margeaux, Martine, and I had a private audience with President Obama. He greeted each of us warmly, and we chatted for a few minutes. I reflected back on Dutch's saying to a reporter that it wasn't possible for a Negro boy to even dream of becoming mayor. And here were Dutch's children and grandchildren meeting the president of the United States of America, who was black, like us.

I was slightly self-conscious greeting the president from a wheelchair. After expressing how proud I was of him, I said pointedly, "You know, Mr. President, I broke my ankle at your house."

He said, "I am so sorry. You are not going to sue me, are you?"

I smiled. "Of course not."

It turned out that no bone was broken, but the ankle was so severely sprained that it was hard to tell. Whatever my injury, I was not suffering much pain at that moment. I was just grateful to be with the leader of the free world. And that world seemed a bit freer to me on that particular day.

EPILOGUE

Flood and Fire

On June 17, 2011, the telephone woke me from a deep sleep. I glanced at the clock. It was 5:30 A.M. in Baton Rouge. I picked up the phone and heard Marc's urgent voice: "Mom, Harrison Avenue is on fire."

"In our block?" I asked.

"Our house!"

Marc was in New York but had learned of the fire almost immediately. His wife, Michelle, had worked as a news anchor in New Orleans and still had connections with the media. A former colleague had called her with the news.

I spoke with him a minute or two more. He told me that Jacques and Monique were on the scene, and that I should wait to hear from them. I hung up the phone, then lay there trying to get my bearings.

It had been six years since Hurricane Katrina flooded my home on Bayou St. John. The entire first floor and its contents were destroyed. The hurricane had also damaged Julie's and Jacques's houses and totally destroyed Monique's. The disaster disrupted my children's lives and careers

236

and stalled their hopes and plans. Still, they had somehow managed to get on their feet again.

After Katrina, Jacques found his niche in community activism, as an advocate for people outside of the standard support system who needed health care, decent housing, and social justice. In this pursuit, he was using his considerable skills as journalist, researcher, grant writer, and negotiator. His deft political skills, learned at the kitchen table and in political campaigns with his father and brother, were an asset to his work. Eventually, he would be deeply involved in organizing aid to the people of earthquake-stricken Haiti and would serve as a monitor of elections in Latin America and Africa.

The Katrina disaster ended Julie's position as director of disease management at Tulane University Medical School and Charity Hospital. Eventually, she took a position as medical director for Blue Cross Blue Shield of Louisiana while continuing to raise her two children. Believing that healing and service go hand in hand, she became involved in health-related service organizations and became the corporate medical and marketing director for a Medicare management company.

Monique had clerked for three years in civil district court and the Louisiana Court of Appeals, then practiced law for several years with local firms. When Hurricane Katrina wrecked her house (she rebuilt three years later), she changed her professional course and entered the race for judge in the First City Court. She was elected without opposition. She chose that court because many defendants who came before it had no legal representation. My daughter has always believed that everyone should be respected and their dignity upheld, no matter what their circumstances.

Cheri, along with her husband and two children, had of course sheltered us in Baton Rouge during Katrina and its aftermath. She had searched for a fulfilling career and held several positions before finding a niche at a national bank as community development officer, promoting and enabling people of modest means to buy affordable housing. She became involved in several community organizations, one of which was the Baton Rouge Downtown Development District, an organization critical to the city's progressive initiatives.

Marc was living in New York when Katrina struck. He watched, albeit at a distance, the destruction of the city he had served for two terms as mayor. He subsequently became president and CEO of the National Urban League. This time, his efforts affected people across the country in the areas of education, employment, housing, and health care.

For years after Hurricane Katrina, I was reluctant to return to New Orleans. My neighborhood on Bayou St. John remained deserted. It was hard even to visit the house. Somehow, though, I always knew I would go back. I enjoyed living in Baton Rouge as a temporary refugee, but New Orleans had been my home since I was born. Just two weeks before Marc's phone call, a contractor and his crew had begun the restoration of my home.

I was exhilarated at the prospect of living there again. I hoped to return to New Orleans by December and to celebrate Christmas there with my children and grandchildren. Since Dutch had died on Christmas Eve in 1989, our family had always tried to be together on that day.

I lay in my bed waiting for dawn, and for a call from Jacques or Monique. The Baton Rouge television stations had no news yet of the fire. I was trying to make some sense of the situation while knowing little. My flooded house was now on fire? It seemed unreal. Even when Jacques and Monique called from the scene an hour later—it was daylight by then—the situation seemed surreal. Jacques reported the house was still burning, but the fire department was out in full force fighting the blaze. Even then, it seemed difficult to grasp; I was trying to make sense of a situation that had none to offer.

I kept thinking about how, when we were young, my mother would admonish us kids by telling us we needed to "take inventory." That phrase, which meant something quite simple when I was a child, came to mean something much more substantial as I grew older. At several crucial points in my life, I have had, sometimes painfully, to "take inventory."

When Dutch considered becoming a candidate for the Louisiana legislature, the odds were against him. And if he won, he would have to make substantial professional adjustments. He would have to be at the State Capitol two or more months a year, away from his law practice. But how could he not try? That was what we were about, securing a place at the "American table," having a voice in our race's destiny.

Following Dutch's death, I had to consider my life going forward. After classroom teaching, Xavier University afforded a second, extraordinary career. For 28 years, serving in several administrative positions, I worked with an administration, faculty, and staff, all committed to educating students not just for their professional lives, but for leadership, so they could contribute to creating a more just and humane society. Here, too, I honed my own professional skills—*A House Divided* emerged from Xavier—and I deepened my values under the guidance of President Norman Francis, who set high standards for the entire Xavier community. Xavier would be a place I could continue to grow.

Two years later, though, I was approached about becoming a candidate for mayor. I had privately thought about it, and when support began to swell, I gave it serious thought. I knew I could do it. I had witnessed Dutch doing it. I had a vision for what was needed to move the city forward. The polls indicated that the race was mine to lose. For several days, I pondered whether or not this was the direction I wanted my life to take. I was not yet sixty, and the choice would determine my life for years. I knew it would be a total commitment, I knew the highs and lows of the office, I knew the possible successes in achieving goals, as well as the stresses and disappointments that came with political office. In the end, I decided being mayor of New Orleans was not my destiny.

Months later, Marc, then a Louisiana state senator, decided to enter the race for mayor. As that challenge unfolded, my new role became clear. I would support his candidacy with all my experience. I would use this renewed fervor for my son's aspirations to advocate for justice and equality through the kind of political involvement that had been so much a part of my life with Dutch.

Three and a half years after Marc completed his second term as mayor, in August 2005, Hurricane Katrina visited chaos on my life and on those of Julie, Jacques, and Monique in ways we could never have imagined. Our existence was torn asunder by a natural disaster that could not have been predicted and over which we had no control.

While reconstructing their lives, my children had to keep their psyches intact; I didn't want them to worry about me and my recovery. They had their own challenges. I thought, *I will be fine.* And I was. What kept things in perspective for me during this nightmare was thinking about the victims of Katrina who had lost everything—lost family members, lost homes and jobs—and had no means to recover. I would recover. But those people had become so fragile that their lives would never be the same. I don't mean to overstate this, but in some ways I counted myself lucky.

I had retired from Xavier two months before Katrina and was looking forward to spending more time with my growing family—grandchildren were appearing yearly—and with friends. In a corner of my mind, I wanted to write a memoir, but it was not an urgent desire. After a month of lodging with Cheri and her family, I decided to live temporarily in Baton Rouge, where I could enjoy, at close range, four of my grandchildren and be near enough to New Orleans to drive over for meetings and oversee the restoration of my home. I thought I would wait for my neighbors to return. So I remained in Baton Rouge for five years, waiting and working on my writing. Still, my neighborhood remained deserted.

In 2010, I decided it was time for me to go home. Now, my house was on fire.

Later that day, I read the news report: "The Morial family home, where two of New Orleans' mayors have lived, was the scene of a four-alarm fire before dawn. The extent of the damage is not yet known. Flames coming out of the roof were reported at about 4 A.M. Over 60 firemen fought the fire until dawn. Several were treated for heat exhaustion."

❧

Three weeks after the flames were doused, I stood in front of my ravaged home. All of the memorabilia—photographs, letters, films, documents—that would have conjured up the many years of my family's history were gone. I looked around the yard and thought about all the peach trees I had grafted. They were gone, too.

My father loved a beautiful garden, just as Mother did. Late in life, when his work days were waning, he reverted to his farming origins and spent much of his free time in the garden planting flowers. His pride and joy were his roses, about thirty plants, which he cultivated with care. My parents' garden was filled with flowers year-round. Whenever I needed to make a floral arrangement for a dinner or reception, I could always count on getting seasonal flowers from their yard.

By that time, he and my mother lived three houses down from us on the bayou. They built their home seven years before we built ours, so they were neighbors from the beginning. One day, my father brought a young peach tree to plant in my backyard. He had grown the sapling from a seed from his own peaches. He knew I loved trees, and the gift pleased Dutch and the children greatly.

"How about here, behind your room, Marc and Jacques? All of you will be able to see it from the balconies off your bedrooms," Dad said.

And that was where we planted it. It was just about three feet tall, and I wondered if it would make it. We gave it fertilizer and frequent watering, then watched. Make it, it did! It thrived for twenty years, and only then did it begin to fail. I had it pruned and fertilized, but it still struggled. Each year, though, the blossoms came and later the peaches, now not so tasty, but the birds didn't seem to notice and still feasted on them. By then, my father had been gone for almost twenty years, and the tree had deep sentimental meaning for all of us. I didn't want to lose it and had an idea. I decided to try to graft six plants from the failing tree, one for each of my five children to plant in their yards, and one for me to plant anew.

Only three of the saplings made it. I nurtured each one, waiting for them to get big and healthy enough to transplant. But then Hurricane Katrina came. The peach trees perished in the winds and flood.

In thinking about those lost saplings, I recalled the words Marc spoke at Dutch's funeral, about his leaving five strong branches—his five children—behind. They were our grafts, his and mine, and they survived. After the flood and after the fire, they had come to my rescue, providing refuge, taking care of my fluctuating health, digging out the flooded house on the bayou, and, at the last, standing guard in the night while the flames scorched the upper floor of our home. I had convinced myself that I was the one who had to be strong for them. But they, each in their turn, had been strong for me—strong for Dutch, too.

I cherish the memories Dutch and I shared and still bring them to mind. I had no way of knowing how challenging and fulfilling my life alone would be. My one continuing sorrow is that Dutch did not live to see his children achieve success in their careers, and to see how brightly they carry on his legacy of service in their personal and professional lives. That gift was left for me.

My parents, Eudora and Dr. C. C. Haydel Sr.
Author's Collection

My abiding gratitude to my parents who set high standards and instilled in us a sense of purpose in life, who taught us to share our talents and time in helping those who needed support. And also to my sister Jean who enriched my life with her courage, strength, and joie de vivre and my brothers C. C. and Glenn who, during good times and hard times, always shared their love and support.

Sybil Morial's family at Gallier Hall on the occasion of Monique Morial's investiture as judge. Back: Michelle Miller Morial and Marc Morial, Juan and Julie Morial Cruz, Monique Morial, Cheri and Verge Ausberry, Jacques Morial, and Kemah Dennis-Morial, Front: *Mason Morial, Martine and Mathieu Cruz, the author, Austin Ausberry, Margeaux Morial, and Jaiden Ausberry. In the background are portraits of the late Dutch Morial and Marc Morial*

BERNIE SAUL, PHOTOGRAPHER

Index